THE
MOST IMPORTANT THING
YOU'LL EVER STUDY

OTHER CROSSWAY BOOKS BY STARR MEADE:

Keeping Holiday

Mighty Acts of God: A Family Bible Story Book

God's Mighty Acts in Creation *(forthcoming)*

God's Mighty Acts in Salvation *(forthcoming)*

THE | MOST IMPORTANT
THING YOU'LL EVER STUDY

A SURVEY OF THE BIBLE

VOLUME 5:
ANSWER KEY

starr meade

CROSSWAY

WHEATON, ILLINOIS

The Most Important Thing You'll Ever Study: A Survey of the Bible, vol. 5: Answer Key
Copyright 2010 by Starr Meade
Published by Crossway
        1300 Crescent Street
        Wheaton, Illinois 60187

Cover design: Brand Navigation, LLC
First printing 2010
Printed in the United States of America

Scripture quotations are from the ESV® Bible (*The Holy Bible, English Standard Version*®), copyright © 2001 by Crossway. Used by permission. All rights reserved.

Volume 5 ISBN: 978-1-4335-2702-9

Full Set:
Trade paperback ISBN:	978-1-4335- 1182-0
PDF ISBN:	978-1-4335- 1183-7
Mobipocket ISBN:	978-1-4335- 1184-4
ePub ISBN:	978-1-4335- 2397-7

Old Testament Set vols. 1 & 2:
Trade paperback ISBN:	978-1-4335- 2024-2
PDF ISBN:	978-1-4335- 2025-9
Mobipocket ISBN:	978-1-4335- 2026-6
ePub ISBN:	978-1-4335- 2027-3

Old Testament Set with Answer Key vols. 1, 2, & 5
Trade paperback ISBN:	978-1-4335- 2028-0
PDF ISBN:	978-1-4335- 2029-7
Mobipocket ISBN:	978-1-4335- 2030-3
ePub ISBN:	978-1-4335- 2031-0

New Testament Set vols. 3 & 4
Trade paperback ISBN:	978-1-4335- 2032-7
PDF ISBN:	978-1-4335- 2042-6
Mobipocket ISBN:	978-1-4335- 2043-3
ePub ISBN:	978-1-4335- 2044-0

New Testament Set with Answer Key vols. 3, 4, & 5
Trade paperback ISBN:	978-1-4335- 2045-7
PDF ISBN:	978-1-4335- 2046-4
Mobipocket ISBN:	978-1-4335- 2047-1
ePub ISBN:	978-1-4335- 2048-8

Crossway is a publishing ministry of Good News Publishers.

CH	23	22	21	20	19	18	17	16	15
15	14	13	12	11	10	9	8	7	6	5	4

To all parents who are diligent in giving their children
a thorough knowledge of God's Word.

Contents

Volume 1: The Old Testament

Test 1
Books of the Bible and General Information

Short answer.

1. Book.

2. a. Read b. Study

3. God.

4. Intention.

5. Change our beliefs when they disagree with it; obey it.

6. Our sin prevents us from spiritually understanding the Bible.

7. God has given believers the Holy Spirit to enable them to understand his Word.

8. The Law.

9. Moses.

10. The Israelites enter the Promised Land.

11. Genesis, Exodus, Leviticus, Numbers, Deuteronomy.

12. The next division is history.

13. Joshua, Judges, Ruth, 1 and 2 Samuel, 1 and 2 Kings, 1 and 2 Chronicles, Ezra, Nehemiah, Esther.

14. Poetry: Job, Psalms, Proverbs, Ecclesiastes, Song of Solomon.

15. Major Prophets: Isaiah, Jeremiah, Lamentations, Ezekiel, Daniel.

16. Minor Prophets: Hosea, Joel, Amos, Obadiah, Jonah, Micah, Nahum, Habakkuk, Zephaniah, Haggai, Zechariah, Malachi.

17. The books of the major prophets are larger (or longer).

18. "Minor" in "minor prophets" means smaller (or shorter).

19. The Gospels.

20. Matthew, Mark, Luke, John.

21. Like a biography, a Gospel tells of the life of Jesus; unlike a biography, most of its focus is on a small portion of Jesus' life and teachings. A great deal of space is given to telling of his death, and the story goes on after his death with the account of his resurrection and things Jesus did afterward.

22. The next division is history; its only book is Acts.

23. Epistles: Romans, 1 and 2 Corinthians, Galatians, Ephesians, Philippians, Colossians, 1 and 2 Thessalonians, 1 and 2 Timothy, Titus, Philemon, Hebrews, James, 1 and 2 Peter, 1, 2, and 3 John, Jude; Prophecy: Revelation.

24. An epistle is a letter.

25. The apostles (or people who worked closely with them) wrote the New Testament epistles to (relatively) new churches.

26. The main purpose of the last book of the Bible was to encourage persecuted Christians.

Genesis: Part 1

1. Important things whose beginnings are described in Genesis:

   the created universe 1:1–2:3;

   man and woman, made in God's image 2:4–7;

   marriage 2:18–25;

   sin 3:1–7;

   death and suffering 3:8–19;

   God's promise of a Savior from sin 3:15;

   enmity between God and his people and Satan and those who follow him 3:15;

   different languages 11:1–9;

   God's chosen people 12:1–3;

   God's covenant of grace 3:15; 12:1–3; 15:1–21.

2. 2:4.	5. 10:1.	8. 25:12.	11. 37:2.
3. 5:1.	6. 11:10.	9. 25:19.	
4. 6:9.	7. 11:27.	10. 36:1.	

Genesis 1–2

Genesis 1–2

1. "In the beginning."

2. God existed before anything else.

3. Light (day and night).

4. Sea and sky.

5. Dry land and plant life.

6. Sun, moon, stars.

7. Birds and fish.

8. Animals and people.

9. "And God said, 'Let there be light,' and there was light."

10. The words occur eight times.

11. On the seventh day, God rested.

12. God blessed the seventh day and made it holy.

13. These words occur five times.

14. God was looking at "everything that he had made."

15. ". . . his own image."

16. God told man to subdue the earth.

17. God gave man dominion "over the fish of the sea and over the birds of the heavens and over every living thing that moves on the earth."

18. The one thing God said was "not good" was the fact that the man was alone. He solved this problem by creating the woman.

Genesis 3–5

Genesis 3–5

1. Adam could eat from all the trees but one.

2. In that day, Adam would surely die.

3. No.

4. The one who would come from the woman would bruise the Serpent's head.

5. The Serpent would bruise that person's heel.

6. ". . . in the likeness of God."

7. Adam fathered a son "in his own [Adam's] likeness, after his [Adam's] image."

8. He died.	11. He died.	14. Enoch walked with God.
9. He died.	12. He died.	15. He died.
10. He died.	13. He died.	

Genesis 6–11

Genesis 6–11

1. Man's wickedness was great and every intention of the thoughts of man's heart was only evil continually.

2. Noah found favor in the eyes of the Lord.

3. Noah was righteous and blameless and walked with God.

   Noah was righteous **because** he found favor with God.

4. God promised that he would never again destroy all living things with a flood.

5. No.

6. Noah became drunk; Ham mocked his father.

7. No, because God gave Noah every moving thing that lives for food.

8. Yes, because man is made in the image of God.

9. People spoke one language.

10. People were building a tower (1) to make a name for themselves and (2) to keep from being scattered.

11. "Babel" is appropriate because it sounds like the Hebrew for "confused," and the Lord confused people's languages.

12. People in Acts 2 who spoke many languages could understand each other.

13. At Babel, people sought glory for themselves.

14. In Acts 2, people gave glory to God.

15. Divided.

16. United.

Test 2
The Garden of Eden to the Tower of Babel

Multiple choice.

1. b	**4.** b	**7.** d
2. a	**5.** b	**8.** a
3. d	**6.** d	**9.** d

Short answer.

10. First day: light

    Second day: sea and sky

    Third day: land, plants

    Fourth day: sun, moon, stars

    Fifth day: birds and fish

    Sixth day: animals and people

11. The Lord Jesus Christ; Satan bruised his heel when Christ died on the cross.

12. Man has dominion over the earth; man knows the difference between right and wrong; man can create; man can think and reason; man can communicate; man can know, love, and worship God.

Genesis: Part 2

Genesis 12–24

Genesis 12–24

1. God told Abram to leave his country and his father's house and go to the land God would show him.

2. God promised to give Abram's offspring the land where the Canaanites were living.

3. God promised to make a great nation of Abram.

4. God promised blessing to all the families of the earth through Abram.

5. Abram lied to the Egyptians, saying Sarai was his sister and not his wife, because he was afraid someone would want her and kill him to get her.

6. Abram complained that he had no children.

7. God promised Abram as many descendants as there are stars in the sky at night.

8. "And he believed the LORD, and he counted it to him as righteousness."

9. The smoking fire pot and the flaming torch passed between the pieces.

10. No.

11. Sarai suggested that Abram have a child with Sarai's maid, Hagar.

12. Abram named the child Ishmael.

13. Abram was 99 years old when God appeared to him.

14. Abram's name was changed to Abraham, which means "father of a multitude."

15. The heart of God's covenant with his people are the words ". . . and I will be their God."

16. Sarai's name was changed to Sarah.

17. Sarah was 90 years old when God said she would have a baby within a year.

18. Abraham was 100 years old when Sarah gave birth to their son.

19. The baby was named Isaac, which means "he laughs."

20. Abraham had waited for so long for this son, but, even more importantly, this was the child through whom God had said all the promises would be fulfilled. If Isaac were dead, how could God's promises be kept?

21. God uses the phrases "... your son, your only son Isaac, whom you love. . . " to describe Isaac.

22. Abraham's answer was, "God will provide for himself the lamb for a burnt offering."

23. They saw a ram caught in the bushes.

24. Abraham named the place, "The LORD will provide."

25. God had told Abraham to go to a mountain God would show him in the land of Moriah.

Genesis 25–36

Genesis 25–36

1. Rebekah was told, "The older shall serve the younger."

2. Esau traded his birthright for a bowl of lentil stew.

3. Isaac intended to give the blessing to Esau.

4. Rebekah wanted the blessing to go to Jacob.

5. Isaac was blind from old age.

6. Jacob told Isaac, "I am Esau your firstborn."

7. Rebekah had put goatskins on Jacob's hands and neck, so he would feel hairy like Esau.

8. Esau planned to kill Jacob.

9. Rebekah wanted Jacob to find a wife who was not one of the Hittite neighbors.

10. The reason Jacob left was in order to flee from Esau until Esau got over his anger.

11. In his dream, Jacob saw a ladder with angels going up and down on it.

12. God was at the top of the ladder.

13. Jesus refers to "the angels of God ascending and descending" in verse 51.

14. The Lord Jesus Christ is the true access for sinful man to God.

    (Answers will vary according to translations used.)

15. "The land on which you lie I will give to you and to your offspring."

16. "Your offspring shall be like the dust of the earth. . ."

17. ". . . In you and your offspring shall all the families of the earth be blessed."

18. Be with him and keep him.

19. Bring him back.

20. He had done what he'd promised.

21. Rachel.

22. Seven.

23. Leah.

24. Jacob married Rachel and worked seven more years.

25. *Father:* Jacob.

26. *Mom #1:* Leah. *Her sons:* Reuben, Simeon, Levi, Judah, Issachar, Zebulun.

27. *Mom #2:* Rachel. *Her sons:* Joseph, *Benjamin.

28. *Mom #3:* Bilhah. *Her sons:* Dan, Naphtali.

29. *Mom #4:* Zilpah. *Her sons:* Gad, Asher.

30. Esau was on his way to meet Jacob.

31. Jacob admitted that he was not worthy of the least of all God's deeds of love and faithfulness toward him.

32. Jacob reminded God of this promise: "I will surely do you good, and make your offspring as the sand of the sea, which cannot be numbered for multitude."

33. Jacob wrestled with a man.

34. The opponent said Jacob had wrestled with God.

35. Jacob would not let go until his opponent gave him a blessing.

36. Yes, God blessed Jacob.

37. God changed Jacob's name to Israel.

38. At Bethel, God promised Jacob: Nations and kings would come from Jacob; the land he had given to Abraham and Isaac he would give to Jacob and to his offspring.

Genesis 37–50

Answers regarding Joseph's feelings in his "journal entries" will vary. The basic events for each passage were:

1. Joseph dreamed his brothers bowed to him.

2. Joseph's brothers sold him and he became a slave in Egypt.

3. Potiphar's wife lied about Joseph and he was imprisoned.

4. Joseph interpreted the dreams of two fellow prisoners and was right.

5. Joseph interpreted Pharaoh's dreams and was made a ruler.

6. Joseph prospered and Egypt prospered under Joseph.

7. Joseph's brothers went to Egypt to find food during the famine.

8. The families would have died out.

9. God's promise could not have been kept.

10. The brothers were dismayed, because Joseph had great power now and could get revenge.

11. Joseph said God had sent him to Egypt, to preserve life.

12. Joseph said God had preserved a remnant (of his people, those who had received the blessings and the covenant) and had kept alive many survivors.

13. Joseph meant that God had been the ultimate cause behind his going to Egypt.

14. Joseph wanted Jacob and his descendants to come to Egypt because there were still five years of famine left.

15. Jacob and all his family went to Egypt after God told Jacob it was the right thing to do.

16. Joseph's brothers were afraid that now Joseph would get his revenge on them.

17. Joseph said his brothers had meant evil against him.

18. He said God had meant good.

19. Joseph said God had brought about the keeping of many people alive through the brothers' evil intentions.

Test 3
God's Covenant of Grace

Identify.

1. Isaac.
2. Abraham.
3. Abraham.
4. Sarah.
5. Jacob.

6. Isaac.
7. Jesus.
8. Ishmael.
9. Isaac.
10. Jacob.

11. Joseph.
12. Jacob.
13. Adam.
14. God.
15. Joseph.

16. Jacob.
17. Jesus.
18. Isaac.
19. Esau.

Multiple choice.

20. b
21. a
22. d

23. c
24. c
25. d

26. d
27. e
28. d

29. a
30. c

Fill in the blank.

31. Ladder; angels.
32. Lied.
33. Seven; Rachel; Leah.

34. Save lives.
35. Bless me.
36. Grace.

Exodus

Exodus
1–6

Exodus 1–6

1. The bush was on fire, but it did not burn up.

2. God told Moses to take off his shoes, because the ground was holy.

3. God wanted Moses to go to Pharaoh and bring God's people out of Egypt.

4. God gave his name as "I AM WHO I AM" or "I AM."

5. My Lord.

6. LORD.

7. Pharaoh said, "Who is the LORD, that I should obey his voice?" and "I do not know the LORD."

8. The Egyptians would know that he was the LORD.

9. God had not made himself known to them by his name the LORD.

10. His people would know that he was the Lord their God.

Exodus
7–12

Exodus 7–12

1. The water was turned to blood.

2. This was true in the rivers, canals, ponds, pools, and all vessels that could hold water.

3. The second plague was frogs.

4. They were in houses, in bedrooms, on beds, in ovens, in kneading bowls.

5. The third plague was gnats.

6. They said, "This is the finger of God."

7. The fourth plague was flies.

8. God's people lived in Goshen.

9. There would be no flies in Goshen.

10. The fifth plague was a plague on all the livestock.

11. None of the Israelites' livestock died.

12. The sixth plague was boils.

13. Pharaoh's magicians could not even stand before Moses.

14. The seventh plague was hail.

15. It struck down everything alive in the field, man or beast, and struck down every plant and broke every tree.

16. There was no hail in Goshen, where the Israelites lived.

17. The eighth plague was locusts.

18. Pharaoh's servants said, "Let the men go . . . Egypt is ruined."

19. The ninth plague was three days of darkness.

20. There was light in the house of the Israelites.

21. The tenth plague was the death of all firstborn sons.

22. Pharaoh.

23. Pharaoh.

24. The Lord.

25. Pharaoh.

26. The Lord.

27. The Lord.

28. God hardened Pharaoh's heart so God could show his power (through all the plagues) and God's name would be proclaimed in all the earth.

29. The Passover lamb was to be a male sheep or goat, one year old, without defect.

30. All the Passover lambs were to be killed at twilight.

31. The Israelites were to paint some of the lamb's blood on their doorposts and the lintels of their houses.

32. The meat was to be roasted and eaten.

33. Leftovers were to be burned.

34. God would pass through Egypt and strike down every firstborn male.

35. God would pass over that house.

36. No Israelite was to go out of the door of his house.

37. The destroyer.

38. Children.

39. God struck down all the firstborn males in Egypt at midnight.

40. There were no Egyptian houses without someone dead.

41. Christ is called our Passover lamb.

Exodus 13–18

Exodus 13–18

1. God led the Israelites by a pillar of cloud in the daytime and by a pillar of fire at night.

2. The Israelites responded in fear and panic.

3. God had hardened Pharaoh's heart so he would follow the Israelites. God would receive glory and all the Egyptians would know God was the Lord.

4. God caused the waters of the Red Sea to part and stand, piled up on either side, so the Israelites were able to cross on dry land. When the Egyptians followed in their chariots, God caused their wheels to stick and caused the Egyptians to panic. Then the waters returned to their place, drowning the Egyptians.

5. The people feared the Lord and believed in him and in Moses as his servant.

6. The main miracle workers in the Bible are Moses, Elijah, Elisha, Jesus, Peter, and Paul.

7. The water was too bitter to drink.

8. Throw into the water a log he showed him.

9. The waters became sweet.

10. The Lord revealed himself to the people as "The Lord, your healer."

11. There was nothing to eat.

12. The Lord would rain down bread from heaven and would send meat as well.

13. In the evening, quail came up and covered the camp. In the morning, there was bread on the ground.

14. The people called the bread "manna."

15. The bread became wormy and smelled bad when anyone gathered more than he needed.

16. It did not fall on the Sabbath.

17. The people had no water.

18. God would stand on the rock at Horeb. Moses was to strike the rock and water would come from it.

19. Water flowed from the rock for the people to drink.

20. God was on the rock.

21. "The Rock was Christ."

Exodus 19–24

Exodus 19–24

1. The Israelites would be God's treasured possession among all peoples, a kingdom of priests to him, and a holy nation.

2. The Israelites were to obey God and keep his covenant.

3. The mountain's name was Mount Sinai.

4. The animal would be put to death.

5. The people saw lightning and a thick cloud, and the mountain wrapped in smoke. They heard thunder and a very loud trumpet. They felt the earth quake and the mountain tremble.

6. "I am the LORD your God."

7. ". . . who brought you out of the land of Egypt, out of the house of slavery."

8. Have no gods but God.

9. Make no images to worship.

10. Honor God's name.

11. Keep the Sabbath.

12. Honor your parents.

13. Do not murder.

14. Do not commit adultery.

15. Do not steal.

16. Do not lie.

17. Do not covet.

18. The Israelites said they would obey all God's commands.

Exodus 25–34

Exodus 25–34

1. God gave Moses two tablets of stone, written on by the finger of God.

2. The people asked Aaron to make gods for them.

3. Aaron proclaimed a feast for the Lord.

4. God said he would consume the people in his wrath, and make a great nation of Moses instead.

5. Moses said God should turn from his anger at the Israelites so the Egyptians would not think he had led his people from Egypt to kill them. Moses also said God should remember his promises.

6. Moses threw down the tablets and broke them, burned the calf and ground it into powder, then making the Israelites drink it, and called on the Levites to kill people with the sword.

7. Moses asked God to forgive the people, and said if God would not, God should blot Moses out of his book too.

8. "For there is one God, and there is one mediator between God and men, the man Christ Jesus."

Exodus 35–40

1. The ark of the covenant was made of acacia wood, overlaid with gold.

2. The testimony God gave Moses (the Ten Commandments) was to be kept in the ark.

3. The mercy seat was made of pure gold.

4. On both ends of the mercy seat were cherubim.

5. God would meet with his people from the mercy seat.

6. The priest was to offer incense on the incense altar every morning and every evening.

7. Nothing else was to be burnt on it—not grain offerings or burnt offerings or even unauthorized incense.

8. The priests were to wash with water.

9. They would do this in the bronze basin.

10. Aaron and his sons were the first priests, and then Aaron's descendants after him.

11. The people did according to all that the Lord had commanded Moses.

12. 39:42; 39:43; 40:16; 40:19; 40:21; 40:23; 40:25; 40:27; 40:29; 40:32.

13. The glory of the Lord filled the tabernacle.

14. The cloud was taken up from the tabernacle when it was time to go.

Test 4
Escape from Egypt

Multiple choice.

1. b	4. c	7. a	10. b
2. d	5. d	8. b	11. e
3. d	6. e	9. c	

Short answer.

12. Judgment.

13. Manna was food God provided for the Israelites. It fell from the sky daily.

14. Mount Sinai.

15. Jesus.

16. God; Israel.

17. Jesus took the punishment our sins deserved.

18. Jesus changes our hearts.

19. Tabernacle.

20. The Ten Commandments:

Have no gods but God.

Make and worship no graven images.

Honor God's name.

Keep the Sabbath.

Honor your parents.

Do not kill.

Do not commit adultery.

Do not steal.

Do not give false testimony.

Do not covet.

Matching.

21. D   **22.** A   **23.** B   **24.** C

Leviticus

Leviticus 1–10

Leviticus 1–10

1. A bull, a sheep or goat, or turtledoves or pigeons.

2. Fine flour with oil and frankincense; or baked unleavened loaves, wafers, or bread baked on a griddle, all with oil; or fresh roasted ears of grain or corn with oil and frankincense.

3. A cow or bull, or a sheep or goat.

4. A bull.

5. A male goat.

6. A female goat or sheep.

7. Two turtledoves or pigeons.

8. Fine flour.

9. A ram.

10. The person bringing an animal to sacrifice laid his hands upon its head before it was killed.

11. Two lambs were to be offered daily.

12. Nadab and Abihu offered unauthorized fire that God had not commanded.

13. God responded by sending fire to consume them.

14. "Among those who are near me I will be sanctified, and before all the people I will be glorified."

Leviticus 11–16

1. "Be holy, for I am holy."

2. No priest was ever to enter inside the tabernacle veil, before the ark of the covenant.

3. If a priest were to go in there, he would die.

4. The exception was once a year, on the Day of Atonement.

5. Before making atonement for the people, the high priest had to kill a bull and use its blood to make atonement for himself and for his household.

6. The high priest killed the first goat and sprinkled its blood on the mercy seat.

7. The priest laid his hands on the head of the other goat, confessed the sins of the people, then sent it away into the wilderness, where it was to "bear all their iniquities . . . to a remote area."

Leviticus 17–27

1. Sabbath.

2. Once a week.

3. One day.

4. Because of the covenant the Israelites had with God.

5. They did no work.

6. Passover.

7. Once a year.

8. One day.

9. Feast of Unleavened Bread.

10. Once a year.

11. Seven days.

12. The first and last days, the Israelites did no work. All seven days, they ate unleavened bread and offered food offerings.

13. Feast of Firstfruits.

14. The people brought a sheaf of the firstfruits of their harvest to wave before the Lord. This was before they ate any of the produce of their crops. They offered other offerings as well.

15. Feast of Weeks.

16. The people offered a grain offering—loaves of bread—with seven lambs and a bull, plus a male goat and two more lambs.

17. Feast of Trumpets.

18. Annually.

19. The people were to proclaim a memorial with blasts of a trumpet, and present a food offering to the Lord and do no ordinary work.

20. Day of Atonement.

21. Annually.

22. To make atonement for the people before the Lord their God.

23. Feast of Booths (or Tabernacles).

24. Eight days.

25. Sabbath Year.

26. Every seventh year.

27. The people were not to sow, plant, reap, or in any way work their land, but were to let it rest.

28. Jubilee.

29. Every fiftieth year.

30. At the beginning of each month.

31. The law is only a shadow of the good things to come.

32. The law and its sacrifices could never make perfect those who drew near.

33. The sacrifices reminded people of sin.

34. It is impossible for the blood of bulls and goats to take away sins.

35. The priests repeatedly offered the same sacrifices every day.

36. The sacrifices could never take away sins.

37. Christ offered a single sacrifice.

38. After Christ had offered his sacrifice, he sat down at the right hand of God.

39. Christ's offering perfected for all time those who are being sanctified.

Numbers

1. Lists of numbers are found in chapters 1, 2, 3, 4, 26.

Numbers 1–10

Numbers 1–10

1. Moses and Aaron were to list all males, twenty years old and older.

2. Go to war.

3. This new census implied that the people were to fight for the Promised Land.

4. A cloud was always over the tabernacle.

5. By night, it appeared like a fire.

6. The Israelites knew when to travel because the cloud would lift from over the tent.

7. They knew where to camp based on where the cloud stopped.

8. In this way, the people set out and camped at the "command of the LORD."

9. The Israelites were leaving the wilderness of Sinai.

10. They were setting out for the land God had promised them.

Numbers 11–14

Numbers 11–14

1. The people complained that they were tired of manna and wanted meat.

2. God gave the Israelites quail to eat.

3. God also sent them a plague that killed many.

4. Miriam's and Aaron's sin was speaking against Moses, God's appointed leader.

5. God had chosen Moses to lead his people.

6. God struck Miriam with leprosy, from which he healed her when Moses prayed for her, but she had to remain outside the camp for seven days.

7. God told Moses to send twelve spies into the Promised Land, one for each tribe.

8. The spies' good report was that the land was good, flowing with milk, honey, and fruit.

9. The spies' bad report was that the cities were too strong to take and the inhabitants were too big and too strong for the Israelites to fight.

10. Caleb and Joshua disagreed with the majority of the spies, insisting that the Israelites could conquer the people because God would be fighting with them.

11. The Israelites responded with fear and complaining, wanting to return to Egypt, and trying to stone Caleb and Joshua for trusting the Lord.

12. God responded to the Israelites' rebellion by saying he would strike them with pestilence, disinherit them, and make a new nation out of Moses.

13. In Moses' prayer, he told God that the Egyptians and the nations around Israel were watching, knowing God was with Israel, and they would think God was not capable of doing what he had promised; Moses also reminded God that he had described himself as slow to anger and forgiving.

14. God said he would pardon the Israelites, as Moses had asked.

15. God said, "all the earth shall be filled with the glory of the LORD."

16. The unbelieving Israelites would die in the wilderness and not see the Promised Land.

17. Only Joshua and Caleb would enter the land.

18. The children of these Israelites would enter the land, after forty years.

19. The Israelites tried to enter the Promised Land.

20. The Israelites were defeated by the Amalekites and the Canaanites.

Numbers 15–25

Numbers 15–25

1. The sin of Korah, Dathan, and Abiram was rebellion against God's chosen leaders, Moses and Aaron.

2. The earth opened and swallowed these men, and all that belonged to them.

3. Fire came out from the Lord and consumed them.

4. God said he would consume the people.

5. 14,700 people died in the plague.

6. Aaron's rod not only sprouted, but also blossomed and produced almonds.

7. The people's problem was a lack of water.

8. God told Moses to speak to a rock and water would come out.

9. Moses hit the rock.

10. God told Moses he would not be allowed to go into the Promised Land because he had disobeyed.

11. The Israelites defeated the king of Arad.

12. The Israelites had been defeated in this place, because of their rebellion.

13. The Israelites complained about the long route they were traveling, and said they were tired of the manna.

14. God sent fiery serpents that bit the people.

15. The people had to look at the bronze serpent to be healed.

16. The serpent on the pole was a picture of Christ on the cross.

17. The Israelites fought King Sihon and the Amorites. The Israelites won and took the Amorites' cities and settled in them.

18. Og, king of Bashan, attacked Israel and Israel defeated him.

19. The people of Moab were terrified of Israel.

20. God sent an angel with a sword as an adversary to Balaam.

21. Balaam's donkey protected Balaam from the angel.

22. The donkey spoke.

23. Balaam stood up to curse Israel four times.

24. Balaam blessed Israel instead.

25. God does not lie or change his mind.

26. Every time God says something, he does it, or fulfills it.

27. "The Lord their God is with them."

28. 24,000 people died of the plague.

Numbers 26–36

1. The Israelites were to drive out all the inhabitants of the land.

Deuteronomy

Deuteronomy 1–34

1. It was "the fortieth year."

2. The Israelites were in Moab, on the other side of the Jordan.

3. Moses was trying to explain the law.

4. God is the God of his people; God is one.

5. God's people are to love him with all their heart, with all their soul, and with all their might.

6. Jesus said this is the first and greatest commandment.

7. The Israelites were not to make or carve a form representing God because when he spoke to them on Sinai, they heard a voice but saw no form at all.

8. The Israelites must not carve an image or worship a created thing because the Lord their God is a consuming fire and a jealous God.

9. If the Israelites disobeyed, they would be destroyed, driven from the land, and scattered among the nations.

10. When they repented, they would return to God and obey his voice.

11. God is merciful; he will not leave or destroy his people or forget the covenant he made with them.

12. Israel would be a wise and understanding nation if they kept and did the statutes and rules God had given them.

13. Other nations would be impressed by how wise and understanding Israel would be.

14. The other impressive thing about Israel was how near their God was to them.

15. Israel had heard the voice of God.

16. Verses 35 and 39 emphasize that there is only one God and no other.

17. God had chosen Israel to be his treasured possession.

18. God had *not* chosen the nation of Israel because they were more numerous than other nations.

19. God chose Israel because he loved them and was keeping the oath he had made to their fathers.

20. Israel's righteousness was *not* a reason God was giving them the land.

21. God had set his heart in love on the fathers of these Israelites.

22. God had chosen their offspring (children) after them above all peoples.

23. Amazing things God is or does for his people, from Moses' song in chapter 33:

    There is none like him;

    He comes to their help;

    He is their dwelling place;

    He supports them forever;

    He thrusts out the enemy before them;

    He provides for them and protects them;

    He saves them;

    He is their shield;

    He gives them victory.

24. The Israelites must completely destroy and consume the Canaanites.

25. The Israelites must not make covenants with the Canaanites, intermarry with them, or pity them.

26. If they did, the Canaanites would be a snare to the Israelites, turning their hearts away from God to other gods.

27. The Israelites were also to destroy all the places where the Canaanites had worshiped false gods, along with their carvings, their idols, their pillars, and their altars.

28. The Israelites were to worship and to bring their offerings only to the place God would choose to dwell and to put his name.

29. The Israelites were to be careful to keep their souls diligently, to obey God's commands, and to make known God's commands to their children and to their children's children; they were to be careful not to forget what they had seen or God's commands.

30. The Israelites were to put God's words: on their hearts, on their hands, between their eyes, on the doorposts of their houses, and on their gates.

31. The Israelites were to discuss God's commands with their children when they sat in the house, when they walked by the way, when they lay down, and when they rose up.

32. The Lord required his people to fear him, walk in all his ways, love him, serve him with all their heart and soul, and keep his commandments and statutes.

33. Joshua was not to fear the Canaanites.

34. The Israelites were to remember what God had done to Pharaoh and the Egyptians.

35. The Israelites were not to dread the Canaanites because God was in their midst, and he is a great and awesome God.

36. God was a consuming fire going before the Israelites; he would destroy and subdue the nations before them.

Test 5
Into the Wilderness

Multiple choice.

1. b	**6.** a	**11.** d	**16.** a
2. a	**7.** a, b	**12.** a	**17.** d
3. a	**8.** a	**13.** c	**18.** e
4. c	**9.** c	**14.** a	
5. d	**10.** a	**15.** e	

Short answer.

19. Jesus said this was the greatest commandment.

Matching.

20. D	**24.** C	**28.** C	**32.** F
21. E	**25.** F	**29.** D	**33.** B
22. H	**26.** B	**30.** E	**34.** A
23. G	**27.** A	**31.** A	**35.** B

36. C	40. B	43. E	46. C
37. D	41. A	44. D	47. A
38. D	42. D	45. A	48. A
39. B			

Joshua

Joshua 1

Joshua 1

1. God appointed Joshua leader.

2. The people committed themselves to following Joshua.

3. "Be strong and courageous" occurs four times.

4. God's promise to be with Joshua/his people occurs at least three times.

5. A form of God's promise to give the people the land occurs at least six times.

6. God told Joshua to be very careful to know and to do all that God had commanded in the law he gave to Moses.

Joshua 2–8

Joshua 2–8

1. Rahab hid the spies.

2. All Canaanites must be killed.

3. Rahab was a prostitute.

4. The people in the land feared the Israelites because God was obviously with them.

5. The waters of the Jordan River parted and God's people crossed on dry land; this was similar to the crossing of the Red Sea when the Israelites left Egypt.

6. God caused this to happen so that the people would know God was with Joshua as he had been with Moses (3:7), so the people would know God was with them and would drive out the Canaanites for them (3:10), so all the peoples of the earth would know the hand of the Lord is mighty, and so the Israelites would fear God forever (4:23–24).

7. When God spoke to Moses from the burning bush, at the beginning of Moses' ministry, God told him to take off his shoes.

8. This commander was on no one's side but the Lord's.

9. The strategy for taking Jericho was this: once a day, for six days, the army was to march around the walls of Jericho, with priests carrying the ark of the covenant and blowing trum-

pets. On the seventh day, the army and priests would do the same thing *seven* times; plus, on the seventh time, all the people would shout.

10. The walls fell down and the Israelites went in and took the city.

11. All people, animals, and things were to be destroyed. The only exceptions were Rahab and her family, items made of silver and gold, and vessels made of bronze or iron; these items were to be put in the Lord's treasury.

12. The Israelites fled before the men of Ai and several Israelites were killed. This was because of Achan's sin in taking some of the forbidden objects from Jericho and keeping them for himself.

13. Achan and his family were stoned to death; they and all he had were burned with fire.

14. Joshua read all the Book of the Law to the people, every word of it.

Joshua 9–12

Joshua
9–12

1. The Gibeonites wanted Israel to think they were from far away because Israel was forbidden by God to make any agreements with or to spare any people of Canaan. The Gibeonites brought food that had gone bad and clothes that had worn out, saying these things had been new when they started out, but had gone bad because the trip was so long.

2. Israel made a covenant with Gibeon, to let them live.

3. The Israelite leaders failed to ask counsel of the Lord.

4. The surrounding kings attacked Gibeon because of its covenant with Israel.

5. In this battle, God threw the enemy soldiers into a panic and he threw large hailstones from heaven on them, which killed more enemy soldiers than Israelite swords did.

6. The sun did not set at its normal time.

7. Verses in Joshua 10:29–39 stating that Joshua destroyed every person or left no one alive are: 30, 32, 33, 35, 37, 39.

8. " . . . just as the LORD God of Israel commanded" (verse 40).

9. " . . . because the LORD God of Israel fought for Israel" (verse 42).

10. " . . . and they struck them until he left none remaining"(11:8); "And they struck with the sword all who were in it, devoting them to destruction; there was none left that breathed" (11:11); "But every man they struck with the edge of the sword until they had destroyed them, and they did not leave any who breathed" (11:14).

11. Joshua took all the land, as God had commanded Moses, and distributed it among the tribes of Israel. The land God had promised to his people as far back as Abraham now belonged to them.

Joshua 13–24

Joshua 13–24

1. Rueben.

2. Gad.

3. Judah.

4. Ephraim.

5. Manasseh.

6. Benjamin.

7. Simeon.

8. Zebulun.

9. Issachar.

10. Asher.

11. Naphtali.

12. Dan.

13. Levi was given no land; the inheritance of Levi was the priesthood.

14. None of Israel's enemies withstood them.

15. Not a word of God's promises failed.

16. "Be very strong to keep and to do all that is written in the Book of the Law of Moses . . ."

17. "Be very careful, therefore, to love the LORD your God."

18. The Israelites must not: turn from the Book of the Law, mix with the nations, serve the gods of the nations, make marriages with the nations, or transgress the covenant.

19. God would be angry with the Israelites, bring evil upon them, and destroy them from the land.

Judges

1. "And the people of Israel did what was evil in the sight of the LORD."

2. "In those days there was no king in Israel."

3. "Everyone did what was right in his own eyes."

Judges 1:1–3:6

Judges 1:1–3:6

1–7. All the tribes listed failed to drive out the inhabitants of the land God was giving them.

8. God would not drive out the enemy inhabitants, but would allow them to be "thorns" in the sides of his people.

9. The Israelites broke God's commands and worshiped idols.

10. God gave them over to their enemies to oppress them.

11. The Israelites were miserable and cried to God, who took pity on them.

12. God raised up a deliverer (judge) for them, freeing them from their enemies.

13. The Israelites returned to their sinful, idolatrous ways.

Judges 3:7–16:31

1. Judge: Othniel.

2. Enemy: Cushan-rishathaim of Mesopotamia.

3. Judge: Ehud.

4. Enemy: Eglon, king of Moab (with the Ammonites and the Amalekites).

5. Judge: Shamgar.

6. Enemy: the Philistines.

7. Judge: Deborah with Barak.

8. Enemy: Jabin, king of Canaan.

9. Shamgar used an oxgoad as a weapon.

10. Deborah and Jael were women.

11. Gideon gave as his reasons for not being able to save Israel the fact that his clan was the weakest in the tribe and he was the youngest in his family.

12. God's answer was that he himself would be with Gideon.

13. The Midianites were like the locusts in abundance; even their camels were too many to count!

14. Gideon's original army was 32,000 men.

15. After the fearful went home, Gideon's army was 10,000 men.

16. After the water test, Gideon's army was 300 men.

17. God wanted so small an army so that it would be clear that the Israelites had not saved themselves by their own strength.

18. Gideon's army broke clay pots hiding torches, so that the light would shine out, at the same time blowing trumpets and shouting.

19. God had filled the hearts of the Midianites with fear of Gideon; they panicked at the commotion and began fighting each other.

20. Abimelech killed his seventy brothers.

21. God was judging Abimelech for killing his brothers.

22. Jephthah led God's people against the Ammonites.

23. Jephthah sacrificed his daughter.

24. The Spirit of the Lord began to stir in Samson.

25. Samson answered, "Get her for me, for she is right in my eyes."

26. The honey came from the carcass of a lion.

27. The Spirit of the Lord rushed upon Samson.

28. Samson used the jawbone of a donkey to kill 1,000 men.

29. Samson could do this because "the Spirit of the LORD rushed upon him."

30. The Lord had left Samson.

31. The dead whom Samson killed at his death were more than those he had killed in his life.

Judges 17–21

Judges 17–21

1. The mother dedicated the money to the Lord to make a carved image with it.

2. The Levite was content to stay with Micah and be his personal priest, serving this carved image.

Ruth

1. The story of Ruth takes place in the days when the judges ruled.

Ruth 1–4

Ruth 1–4

1. Naomi and her husband went to Moab because of a famine in Israel.

2. "Your people shall be my people, and your God my God."

3. Ruth "happened" to come to a field belonging to Boaz who was of the clan of Elimelech (Naomi's husband).

4. Boaz said he had heard of all Ruth had done for Naomi and how she had left her own land and people to come with her mother-in-law.

5. Boaz said the Lord, the God of Israel, under whose wings she had come to take refuge, would reward her.

6. Naomi said Boaz was a close relative of theirs, one of their redeemers.

7. Obed's son was Jesse.

8. Jesse's son was David.

9. In the list of Jesus' ancestors, we see Boaz, Ruth, and Obed (and Jesse and David).

Test 6
Looking for a Leader

Matching.

1. H		**7.** L		**13.** B		**19.** A
2. L		**8.** D		**14.** D		**20.** C
3. E		**9.** E		**15.** F		**21.** H
4. J, K		**10.** K		**16.** K		**22.** A
5. I		**11.** A		**17.** F		**23.** F
6. J		**12.** J		**18.** H		**24.** G

Identify.

25. JD	**29.** JD	**33.** J	**37.** J
26. J	**30.** J	**34.** J	**38.** J
27. J	**31.** JD	**35.** JD	**39.** JD
28. R	**32.** R	**36.** R	

Short answer.

40. God had promised the land to his people as part of his covenant with them; when they were in possession of it, it showed that God had faithfully kept his promises, and the people were in his favor. If they should have to leave it, it would mean God was no longer with them and they were under the covenant curses.

1–2 Samuel

1. The king was to keep a copy of God's law with him.

2. The king was to read in the book of God's law all the days of his life.

3. This was so the king would learn to fear God by keeping his statutes and doing them, so he would not become proud or turn from God's commands.

1 Samuel 1–7

1 Samuel 1–7

1. We see the name "LORD of hosts."

2. Hannah was sad because she had no children.

3. Hannah promised to give her son to the Lord.

4. Hannah named her son Samuel.

5. She left him with Eli the priest.

6. Holy.

7. Rock.

8. The bows of the mighty are broken.

9. The feeble bind on strength.

10. The Lord brings down to Sheol and raises up.

11. The Lord makes poor and makes rich, and brings low and exalts.

12. The pillars of the earth are the Lord's, and he has set the world on them.

13. The Lord guards the feet of his faithful ones.

14. The Lord cuts off the wicked in darkness.

15. Not by might shall a man prevail.

16. God will give strength to his king.

17. God will exalt the power of his anointed.

18. Eli's sons were worthless; they did not know the Lord and treated his sacrifice with contempt.

19. God's message through Samuel was for Eli, about how his house would be punished because of the wickedness of his two sons.

20. The Lord did not allow any of Samuel's words to fall to the ground.

21. All Israel knew Samuel had been established a prophet of the Lord.

22. The word of the Lord was rare.

23. The Lord revealed himself to Samuel, by the word of the Lord.

24. The Israelites carried the ark of the covenant into battle with them.

25. The ark was captured and Eli's sons were killed in battle.

26. The Philistines found Dagon face downward on the ground before the ark.

27. Dagon was on the ground before the ark with his head and hands cut off.

28. The Lord sent tumors on the Philistines.

29. Some foolish Israelites looked inside the ark of the covenant.

1 Samuel 8–10

1 Samuel
8–10

1. The people demanded a king.

2. They wanted a king to judge them and to go out before them and fight their battles.

3. The people wanted to be like the other nations.

4. Saul's father was a man of wealth.

5. Saul was taller than any other Israelite, and more handsome than any other.

6. Samuel anointed Saul king over Israel.

7. Samuel told the people the rights and duties of the king, then wrote them in a book.

1 Samuel 11–15

1 Samuel 11–15

1. Saul offered the sacrifice so the Israelites could go to battle, because, while they waited for Samuel (who was late), the people were becoming more and more fearful and were deserting the army.

2. Saul's kingdom would not continue. It would be given to someone else.

3. God had sought out "a man after his own heart" to be prince over his people.

4. Samuel commanded Saul to kill all the Amalekites and all their animals.

5. Saul disobeyed by sparing the life of the king and by keeping the best animals.

6. God prefers obedience to sacrifices and rich gifts.

7. The Lord rejected Saul as king because Saul had rejected the Word of the Lord.

1 Samuel 16–20

1 Samuel 16–20

1. The Lord told Samuel that men look at someone's outer appearance, but the Lord looks on the heart.

2. Jesse's youngest son, David, had not been invited because he was out caring for the sheep.

3. From the time David was anointed king, the Spirit of the Lord was on him.

4. The Spirit of the Lord left Saul, and an evil spirit tormented him.

5. David entered Saul's service as his armor-bearer.

6. He played the harp when the evil spirit troubled Saul.

7. Saul's first response to David's offer is, "You are not able to go against this Philistine."

8. David said he would defeat the Philistine because the Lord would deliver him.

9. Saul thought David needed armor.

10. Instead, David took five stones and a stick.

11. " . . . the LORD saves not with sword and spear. For the battle is the LORD's . . ."

12. David was having many military successes.

13. Saul began to turn against David because he was jealous of him. Saul was also afraid of David because the Spirit of the Lord was with him, and not with Saul.

14. Jonathan loved David; so did all Israel and Judah.

15. David ran away because Saul's hatred had become so intense that he even tried to kill his own son Jonathan, when Jonathan spoke up for David.

1 Samuel 21–31

1. David hid from Saul in the cave of Adullam.

2. 400 men of those who were in debt or in distress or bitter of soul gathered to be David's men there in the cave.

3. David sent his parents to live in Moab.

4. At Saul's command, Doeg killed 85 priests, then destroyed their families and homes. Saul commanded this because he believed the priests were on David's side, against him (Saul).

5. Saul suddenly took his men and left because a message came that the Philistines had invaded Israel.

6. David's men thought God had brought Saul so David could kill him.

7. David only cut a piece from Saul's robe.

8. David would not hurt Saul because he was the Lord's anointed.

9. It seems that David did not trust Saul's guilty feelings, because David went back to his stronghold, continuing to stay far from Saul.

10. Saul and his men slept so soundly because a deep sleep from the Lord had fallen on them.

11. David expected God's control over all things to play itself out by Saul's death in God's timing, without David's help.

12. Saul admitted he had sinned and seemed truly sorry—but he wasn't!

13. God would not answer Saul by any means at all.

14. Saul had cut off all mediums and necromancers (magicians) from the land, as God's law said should be the case.

15. The message for Saul was that God continued to reject him, that he would lose the battle to the Philistines on the next day, and that he and his sons would be dead by the next evening.

16. This message filled Saul with terror and he had no strength left.

17. Saul killed himself, after being been badly wounded by enemy arrows.

18. Saul's sons and his armor-bearer all died in the same battle.

2 Samuel 1–10; 1 Chronicles 1–19

1. David mourned, wept, and fasted because of Saul's death.

2. The messenger said that he had killed Saul at Saul's request. First Samuel 31 told us that Saul had fallen on his own sword from fear of what the Philistines would do to him.

3. David "rewarded" the messenger by having him executed for killing the Lord's anointed.

4. God told David to go to Hebron.

5. The men of Judah anointed David king over the house of Judah.

6. Ish-bosheth, Saul's son, ruled over the rest of Israel for a time.

7. Saul's house became weaker and weaker; David's house grew stronger and stronger.

8. Some men entered Ish-bosheth's house deceptively, killed him on his bed, and took his head to David.

9. David rewarded the killers by having them killed, and by having their hands and feet cut off and their bodies hung up.

10. The people of Israel said the Lord had said David would be shepherd of God's people Israel, and prince over Israel.

11. David made a covenant with Israel.

12. David became greater and greater because the Lord, the God of hosts, was with him.

13. David knew *the Lord* had established him king over Israel.

14. The Lord had exalted his kingdom for the sake of *his people Israel*.

15. David wanted to build a permanent house for the Lord, to replace the tabernacle tent.

16. God said he would make David a house.

17. David's son would be king after David.

18. David's son would build a house for the Lord.

19. God would establish the throne of David's son forever.

20. God would be a father to David's son.

21. If David's son sinned, God would discipline him.

22. God would never take his steadfast love from David's son.

23. David's throne and David's house would last forever.

24. David and the people were moving the ark with a cart pulled by oxen.

25. When Uzzah touched the ark, God became angry and struck him dead.

2 Samuel 11–15

1. Uriah's wife, Bathsheba, was pregnant with David's child. David had Uriah come home from war, hoping he would spend enough time with Bathsheba that people would think the baby was Uriah's baby.

2. David ordered Joab to place Uriah where the fighting was most intense so he would be sure to die and David could marry Bathsheba.

3. "But the thing that David had done displeased the LORD."

4. Nathan told David, "You are the man!"

5. David responded to Nathan's accusation with, "I have sinned against the LORD."

6. "Behold, I was brought forth in iniquity, and in sin did my mother conceive me."

7. David's only hope for cleansing from sin was for God to cleanse and purify him and to change his heart.

8. David deserved to be cast away from God's presence and to have God remove his Holy Spirit from him (which is what had happened to Saul).

9. God is most pleased with the sacrifice of a heart broken and contrite over sin.

10. Consequences of David's sin: violence (the sword) would never depart from his own house; from within his own house evil would come against David; David's wives would be given to someone else; and David and Bathsheba's child would die.

11. David and Bathsheba's second son was Solomon.

12. Solomon was also called "Jedidiah," because the Lord loved him.

13. Absalom was more handsome than anyone in Israel. There was nothing wrong with any part of his body. He had long, heavy hair that he seemed proud of since, each year when he had it cut, he weighed it.

14. Absalom always listened to people's disputes and took their side, wishing he was king so he could give them the justice they deserved. He also greeted everyone as a friend, not letting them bow to him as royalty.

15. Absalom announced himself to be king in Hebron.

16. David had to flee for his life from his own son, leaving Jerusalem.

17. David prayed that Ahithophel's counsel would be turned to foolishness.

18. David had Hushai return to Jerusalem to pretend to be a counselor for Absalom so that he might be able to give advice against the advice Ahithophel gave.

2 Samuel 16–24; 1 Chronicles 20–29

1. Ahithophel counseled that Absalom attack David immediately while he and his men were tired and discouraged, killing only David.

2. Hushai said that since David and his men were great warriors, Absalom should not attack until he had gathered many more fighting men.

3. Absalom took Hushai's advice.

4. This was because "the LORD had ordained to defeat the good counsel of Ahithophel, so that the LORD might bring harm upon Absalom."

5. Absalom met his end when he was caught by the head (probably his long hair?) in a tree his mule had run under. As he dangled there, Joab and ten men surrounded, struck, and killed him.

6. Absalom had erected a pillar as a monument to himself, so he wouldn't be forgotten.

7. Now Absalom lay in a pit under a large pile of stones.

8. David's response was great and obvious grief.

9. Joab scolded David for making his grief so obvious, since it looked like he only cared about his son, and not all those who had loyally and bravely fought for David.

10. All this upheaval surrounded God's action in coming to save David.

11. David said God enabled him to run against a troop and to leap over a wall.

12. God trained David so that his arms could bend a bow of bronze.

13. Verse 41: God made David's enemies turn their backs to him; verse 44: God delivered David from strife and kept him as head of the nations.

14. David was "the sweet psalmist of Israel."

15. The Spirit of the Lord spoke by David.

16. God incited David.

17. Satan incited David.

18. David's heart (conscience) struck him; he said he had sinned and he asked God to forgive him.

19. David chose three days of pestilence.

20. 70,000 of God's people died.

21. David prayed that God would let his people go, and just punish David and his house.

22. The prophet Gad told David to build an altar and offer sacrifices.

23. God responded to David's plea for Israel by removing the plague from Israel.

24. The angel of the Lord was standing by the threshing floor of Araunah the Jebusite.

Test 7

The Life of King David

Identify.

1. Saul.
2. Samuel.
3. Israelites.
4. Absalom.
5. Saul.
6. Nathan.
7. Saul.
8. David.
9. Samuel.
10. Dagon.
11. Hannah.

12. Uzzah.
13. Israelites.
14. Saul.
15. Absalom.
16. David.
17. Absalom.
18. David.
19. Hannah.
20. Samuel.
21. David.
22. Philistines.

23. The Holy Spirit.
24. Solomon.
25. Hannah.
26. Dagon.
27. Nathan.
28. David.
29. Saul.
30. The Holy Spirit.
31. Saul.
32. David.
33. David.

Fill in the blank.

34. A godly king.
35. Law; prophets.
36. After his [God's] own heart.

37. His son or his descendant.
38. Repentance.
39. Joshua.

Short essay.

40. David was a godly king, "a man after God's own heart," who loved God and was guided by his Word. He courageously fought the enemies of God's people, giving his people victory and safety. He ruled fairly and justly.

41. David's selfish sin with Bathsheba resulted in her husband's murder, dishonor to God, and many bloody consequences in David's own family. These consequences affected all of Israel, as when Absalom temporarily took the throne. David's sin in counting the people resulted in a plague that killed thousands of God's people. David's failure to move the ark of the covenant as the Law required resulted in Uzzah's death. God's people need a king who will never put his own desires over theirs and God's, and who will always do what is right and what is best for the people.

1. God would cut Israel off from the land he had given them.

2. God would cast the temple out of his sight and it would become a heap of ruins.

3. Israel would become a proverb and a byword among all peoples.

4. This had happened because the Israelites had abandoned the Lord their God to serve and worship other gods; for this reason, God had brought disaster on them.

1 Kings 1–11; 2 Chronicles 1–9

1 Kings 1–11; 2 Chronicles 1–9

1. God told Solomon, "Ask what I shall give you."

2. Wisdom.

3. Riches.

4. Honor.

5. Women.

6. Baby.

7. Solomon's solution was to cut the baby in half and give each mother a piece.

8. This showed who the real mother was since the real mother would rather give the baby away than have it killed.

9. The people were in awe of the king because they perceived that the wisdom of God was in him to do justice.

10. God's promise to Abraham of a great nation is seen to be fulfilled in 4:20: "Judah and Israel were as many as the sand by the sea"; God's promise of land to Abraham is seen in verse 21: "Solomon ruled over all the kingdoms from the Euphrates to the land of the Philistines and to the border of Egypt."

11. Things from this passage showing Solomon's wisdom: God gave him wisdom and understanding beyond measure; Solomon's wisdom surpassed the wisdom of all the people of the east and all the wisdom of Egypt; he was wiser than all other men; he was famous in all the nations; he wrote 3,000 proverbs; people came from all nations to hear his wisdom.

12. We see that Solomon's reign was a time of peace and prosperity in these statements:

    "They ate and drank and were happy"; "And Judah and Israel lived in safety, from Dan even to Beersheba, every man under his vine and under his fig tree."

13. Examples of Solomon's wealth include: tribute brought from other nations; all the food for his provisions; all his gold and all that he had that was made from gold; his throne was like

no one else's; silver was considered common; he had a fleet of ships that brought riches and exotic goods; and the people who came to hear his wisdom brought him expensive gifts.

14. Solomon tells Hiram that God had given Solomon rest on every side.

15. Solomon had no adversaries or misfortune.

16. The Lord makes a man's adversaries to be at peace with him when his ways are pleasing to the Lord.

17. When Solomon finished praying, a cloud, which held the glory of the Lord, filled the temple.

18. Solomon asked that God would answer the prayer of the foreigner who came to the temple to pray, so other nations would know God is the true God.

19. Solomon had 700 wives and 300 concubines. These women were from the foreign nations, with whom God had commanded the Israelites not to intermarry. Solomon's wives turned his heart away from the Lord to other gods.

20. The Lord was angry with Solomon; he told him he would tear the kingdom from him and give it to his servant—although not in Solomon's day and not the entire kingdom, for the sake of God's promise to David.

21. God began to raise up adversaries against Solomon.

22. Jeroboam was a diligent servant of Solomon's, over some of the forced labor from Israel.

23. Ahijah tore the cloak into twelve pieces, giving ten pieces to Jeroboam. Ahijah said God would divide the kingdom and make Jeroboam king over ten of the tribes.

24. David's descendants would still be king . . .

25. But over only one tribe.

26. Solomon tried to kill Jeroboam, who had to flee to Egypt.

1 Kings 12:1–14:18; 2 Chronicles 10–13

1 Kings
12:1–14:18;
2 Chronicles
10–13

1. Solomon's son, Rehoboam, became king after him.

2. The people, led by Jeroboam, asked Rehoboam to make their load lighter than it had been under Solomon.

3. The older men told Rehoboam to grant the people's request, so they would serve him gladly.

4. The young men told Rehoboam to be even harder on the people than his father had been.

5. Rehoboam took the advice of the young men.

6. Israel's reaction to Rehoboam's answer was to break away from his rule and make Jeroboam their king.

7. Only Judah remained with Rehoboam.

8. This turn of affairs was brought about by the Lord, to fulfill his word which he had spoken to Jeroboam by Ahijah.

9. Jeroboam set up golden calves in Dan and in Bethel, saying these were the gods who had led Israel out of Egypt.

10. Jeroboam said it was too far for the Israelites to have to go all the way to Jerusalem to worship.

11. Jeroboam was afraid that if the people went to Jerusalem to worship, they would want to return to life under the rule of Rehoboam.

12. Jeroboam's reign was evil; he had priests who were not Levites; he led his people in idol worship.

Can you . . . arrange these in chronological order?

8, 13, 3, 12, 17, 10, 6, 2, 15, 4, 20, 14, 9, 18, 5, 16, 7, 19, 11, 1.

Kings and Chronicles: Part 2

1 Kings 14:19–16:34; 2 Chronicles 14–16

1. Rehoboam did evil in God's sight and provoked God to jealousy with the evil practices of the nations.

2. The next ruler in Judah was Abijam, who "walked in all the sins that his father did before him."

3. God did not take the kingdom away from these kings for David's sake.

4. Foreign altars and high places.

5. Seek the Lord.

6. Keep the law.

7. Rely.

8. Man.

9. You.

10. The LORD defeated.

11. Syria.

12. The Lord's treasury.

13. Putting Hanani in the stocks in prison.

14. Asa also "inflicted cruelties" on some of the people.

15. The Lord.

16. Physicians.

17. 22.

18. Nadab.

19. 2.

20. Baasha.

21. Jeroboam's whole family.

22. 24.

23. Dogs.

24. Birds.

25. Elah.

26. 2.

27. Getting drunk.

28. Assassinated.

29. Zimri.

30. Baasha's whole family.

31. 7 days.

32. Set the palace on fire around him.

33. Omri.

34. 12 years.

35. Samaria.

36. Ahab.

37. Samaria.

38. 22.

39. More evil.

40. Jezebel.

41. Sidon.

1 Kings 17–21

1. Rain.

2. "My word."

3. God sent ravens to bring food to Elijah.

4. God sent Elijah to stay with a widow and her son, and, as long as he stayed with her, her flour and oil never ran out.

5. Elijah raised the widow's son from the dead.

6. The contest was on Mount Carmel.

7. The true god would be the one who would send fire from heaven to burn up the sacrifice.

8. 450 priests of Baal participated.

9. They spent the whole day crying out, limping, dancing, and cutting themselves.

10. No one answered; no one paid attention.

11. Elijah dug a trench around his altar and, three times, he poured so much water on the sacrifice that it soaked it and the wood and the altar, and overflowed the trench.

12. Elijah prayed once.

13. Fire fell from heaven and consumed the sacrifice, wood, stones of the altar, and lapped up all the water in the trench.

14. The people cried, "The LORD, he is God!"

15. Elijah killed the prophets of Baal.

16. Jezebel promised to kill Elijah by the next day.

17. Elijah ran away.

18. Elijah wanted to die.

19. Elijah complained that he had been very jealous for God, but Israel had forsaken God's covenant and had killed all the prophets of God and he alone was left.

20. God was not in the fire, the great wind, or the earthquake.

21. God was in the gentle little breeze.

22. God said he still had 5,000 in Israel who had not bowed the knee to Baal.

23. Ahab wanted a vineyard near his house for a vegetable garden.

24. Naboth wouldn't sell it because it was his inheritance from the Lord.

25. Jezebel came up with a plan for getting the vineyard: hire liars to say Naboth had cursed God and the king, then have Naboth executed and take the vineyard.

26. Elijah met Ahab in Naboth's vineyard.

27. Elijah said dogs would lick up Ahab's blood.

28. Dogs would eat Jezebel.

29. "There was none who sold himself to do what was evil in the sight of the LORD like Ahab."

1 Kings 22—2 Kings 6:23

**1 Kings 22—
2 Kings 6:23**

1. The 400 prophets told Ahab to go ahead and go to battle; he would have victory.

2. Ahab said that Micaiah always prophesied evil about him.

3. Die.

4. A spirit had offered to be a lying spirit in their mouths and God had said, "Go."

5. Ahab dressed like a nobody and encouraged Jehoshaphat to dress like a king, so he would draw the enemy fire away from Ahab.

6. A "certain man drew his bow at random" and hit Ahab in a vulnerable spot in his armor.

7. Dogs licked up Ahab's blood.

8. The word of the Lord.

9. The next king was Ahaziah, son of Ahab.

10. Ahaziah sent messengers to Baal-zebub, god of Ekron.

11. Ahaziah sent fifty armed men to capture Elijah.

12. Elijah called down fire from heaven that destroyed them.

13. The king sent fifty more armed men, and fire from heaven destroyed them.

14. The third captain of fifty humbled himself before Elijah, and God told Elijah to go with him.

15. Jehoram.

16. Elijah went to heaven in a fiery chariot.

17. Elisha asked for a double portion of Elijah's spirit.

18. Elijah dropped his mantle from the chariot for Elisha to pick up.

19. Elisha had the widow borrow oil jars, fill them all from one small jar she had, then sell the oil.

20. Elisha told the Shunammite woman she would have a child—and she did.

21. Elisha brought the child back to life when he died.

22. Naaman was the commander of the Syrian army; he had leprosy.

23. A captive Jewish girl worked for Naaman's wife and told her about Elisha.

24. Naaman was offended that Elisha didn't even see him, just sent a messenger to say, "Go and wash in the Jordan seven times."

25. Naaman said, "I know that there is no God in all the earth but in Israel."

26. Elisha wouldn't take any of the gifts Naaman offered him.

27. Gehazi went after Naaman, and asked for some of the gifts.

28. Gehazi was struck with leprosy.

29. Elisha was revealing all Syria's secret plans to the king of Israel.

30. The servant saw horses and chariots of fire all around Elisha.

31. God struck the Syrian army with blindness, so that they willingly followed Elisha, who took them straight to the king of Israel.

2 Kings 6:24—2 Kings 12

2 Kings
6:24—
2 Kings 12

1. Jehu killed Jehoram.

2. Jezebel was thrown out of the window; when they eventually went to recover her body, it had been eaten by dogs.

3. Jehu also killed King Ahaziah from Judah.

4. Jehu did well to wipe out Baal worship, but he continued in the idol worship Jeroboam had begun in Israel.

Test 8

Israel Divided

Multiple choice.

1. a

2. a, b, c, d

3. c

4. a, c, d

5. d

6. K, C, C, K

Short essay.

7. Israel divided into two kingdoms, Israel in the north and Judah in the south. God had told Solomon he would take most of the kingdom from his descendants because of Solomon's idolatry. Later, a prophet tore a robe into twelve pieces and gave ten pieces to Jeroboam, saying God would give him ten tribes to rule. When Solomon's son Rehoboam became king, his people asked him to rule less harshly than their father had ruled. He refused their request and all but the people from Judah rejected him as king and made Jeroboam king instead.

8. Jeroboam told his subjects that Jerusalem was too far away for them to have to go to worship God, so he set up calves in Dan and Bethel and told the people they could worship there. The truth was that he was afraid that if his people went to Jerusalem, they would decide to have Rehoboam as king again.

Short answer.

9. All the kings in the northern kingdom were wicked.

10. Samaria was the capital of the northern kingdom.

11. The capital of the southern kingdom was Jerusalem.

Identify.

12. Elijah.	**20.** Elijah.	**28.** Elijah.
13. Ahab.	**21.** Jezebel.	**29.** Ahab.
14. Jeroboam.	**22.** Elisha.	**30.** Solomon.
15. Elisha.	**23.** Solomon.	**31.** Jehu.
16. Ahab.	**24.** Jehu.	**32.** Elijah.
17. Elijah.	**25.** Elisha.	**33.** Elijah.
18. Jezebel.	**26.** Jezebel.	**34.** Jezebel.
19. Rehoboam.	**27.** Elijah.	**35.** Solomon.

Kings and Chronicles: Part 3

2 Chronicles 17–22

2 Chronicles 17–22

1. Jehoshaphat.

2. Jehoshaphat walked in David's ways, sought God and walked in his commandments. He didn't seek the Baals, and he didn't follow practices of Israel; therefore, the Lord established the kingdom in his hand. The Lord was with him.

3. Jehoshaphat sent his officials to go through all the cities of Judah with the Book of the Law, teaching.

4. The fear of the Lord fell on the neighboring nations and they made no war against Judah.

5. Jehoshaphat's one bad move was making a marriage alliance for his son with Ahab's daughter.

6. Jehoshaphat brought the people back to the Lord. He appointed judges, priests, and Levites as judges, exhorting them to judge fairly.

7. A large multitude of Moabites, Ammonites, Meunites, and Edomites came against Jehoshaphat.

8. Jehoshaphat set his face to seek the Lord and proclaimed a fast, then prayed.

9. You rule everything and no one can resist you.

10. You drove the former inhabitants out of this land and gave it to Abraham's descendants.

11. There is a temple for you here, where your people call out to you when they're in trouble.

12. You didn't let us attack the Ammonites or the Moabites when we came from Egypt.

13. They reward us by driving out your people from the land you gave them.

14. We're powerless; we don't know what to do; we look to you; please judge them.

15. God told his people to go up against them, but said they wouldn't have to fight; God would be with them and they would see his salvation.

16. As evidence of Jehoshaphat's trust in the Lord, the singers and musicians led his army the next day, praising God.

17. Moab and Ammon fought against Edom, then turned and destroyed each other.

18. The Lord set this ambush.

19. Jehoram's father was Jehoshaphat.

20. Jehoram's father-in-law was Ahab.

21. Jehoram imitated Ahab.

22. Jehoram's wife was Athaliah, the daughter of Ahab.

23. Jehoram killed all his brothers.

24. The Lord sent an incurable disease and Jehoram's bowels came out; he died in great agony.

25. Jehoram's people felt no regret over his death.

26. Ahaziah was the next king in Judah.

27. He ruled one year.

28. Ahaziah's counselor was his mother, and she counseled him to do wickedly.

29. God had ordained Ahaziah's downfall through his visit to the wounded king of Israel.

30. When Ahaziah was visiting in Israel, Jehu wiped out Ahab's family and killed Ahaziah, because Ahaziah was a member of Ahab's family—his grandson.

31. Ahaziah's mother, Athaliah, had all her grandchildren killed so she could be queen.

32. Joash escaped because his aunt and her priest husband Jehoiada hid him in the temple.

33. If Athaliah had succeeded in killing all of her grandchildren, the promises in God's covenant with David would have gone unfulfilled.

34. Athaliah ruled six years.

2 Chronicles 23–26

1. The priest Jehoiada led the uprising to make Joash king.

2. Athaliah was put to death.

3. Joash was seven years old when he became king.

4. Joash did "what was right in the eyes of the Lord" all the days of Jehoiada.

5. Joash initiated and commanded the project of restoring the temple.

6. After Jehoiada died, leaders in Judah talked Joash into abandoning the house of the Lord to serve idols.

7. God sent prophets to bring his people back, but the people paid no attention.

8. Zechariah was Jehoiada's son.

9. He was Joash's cousin.

10. Zechariah's message to Joash was that, because Joash had forsaken the Lord, the Lord had forsaken Joash.

11. Joash responded to Zechariah's message by having him stoned to death in the court of the house of the Lord.

12. The Syrian army had few men; Joash's army was a very great multitude.

13. The Syrians won the battle because Judah had forsaken God.

14. Joash's servants assassinated him, because he had killed Zechariah.

15. Amaziah did what was right in the eyes of the Lord, but not with a whole heart.

16. Amaziah hired 100,000 men from Israel to fight in his army.

17. The problem with that was that the Lord wasn't with Israel; all Judah needed was the Lord.

18. Judah won the battle against Edom (Seir).

19. Amaziah took the idols that hadn't protected Edom from his attack, set them up, and began to worship them.

20. Amaziah silenced the prophet who rebuked him for this.

21. Uzziah became king in Judah next.

22. Uzziah did what was right; he set himself to seek God, he was instructed in the fear of God.

23. Uzziah's reign was, militarily, very strong; he completed successful building projects; farming was prosperous; God prospered him and his fame spread.

24. Uzziah's heart became proud.

25. Uzziah tried to offer incense.

26. Uzziah became leprous, and it lasted until he died.

2 Kings 13–14

2 Kings 13–14

1. Jehoahaz did what was evil in the sight of the Lord, not departing from the sins Jeroboam had introduced.

2. Jehoash did what was evil in the sight of the Lord, not departing from the sins of Jeroboam which he made Israel sin.

3. Jeroboam II did what was evil in the sight of the Lord. He did not depart from the sins of Jeroboam.

Amos

Amos 1–9

Amos 1–9

1. Damascus.

2. Gaza.

3. Tyre.

4. Edom.

5. The Ammonites.

6. Moab.

7. Amos spoke against the sins of Judah.

8. Amos prophesied against Israel.

9. The Israelites told Amos to go home and not prophesy there anymore.

10. Amos prophesied because the Lord told him to.

11. Calamity comes to a city because the Lord has done it.

12. When the Lord God spoke, the prophet had to prophesy.

13. Amos 3 was directed against the people of Israel.

14. Judgment was going to fall on the Israelites because they had not lived up to the privilege of having God as their God and because of their robbery and violence.

15. The altars of Bethel.

16. The wealthy great houses.

17. Israel's enemies would conquer the kingdom.

18. Amos 4 was directed against the "cows of Bashan."

19. They would be judged because they oppressed the poor and thought only about their own pleasure and comfort.

20. They would be taken away with fishhooks.

21. Famine.

22. Drought (lack of rain).

23. Blight, mildew, and locusts to attack crops.

24. Pestilence (or sickness).

25. He had overthrown some of their cities.

26. God's people never returned to him.

27. The people were to prepare to meet their God.

28. God was able to form mountains and create the wind; he was able to reveal to people his thoughts; he was able to make morning darkness and to walk on the highest places of the earth.

29. Amos 5 was directed against the house of Israel.

30. They were corrupting justice and righteousness; they hated truth; they abused the poor and took bribes.

31. Israel would fall with none to raise her up.

32. Both passages begin with the word "woe."

33. Darkness.

34. Light.

35. Gloom.

36. Brightness.

37. Locusts.

38. God relented.

39. Fire.

40. God relented.

41. Wall.

42. Plumb line.

43. Pass by them.

44. Basket of summer fruit.

45. End.

46. The Lord.

47. Altar.

48. Evil.

49. Good.

50. David's.

51. Edom.

52. Nations who are called by my [God's] name.

53. That day.

54. Acts 15:16–17.

Hosea

Hosea 1–14

Hosea 1–14

1. God told Hosea to take a "wife of whoredom."

2. Israel was committing whoredom, or adultery, by forsaking the Lord.

3. The first child was to be named "Jezreel."

4. The second, "No Mercy," and the third, "Not My People."

5. The children of Israel would be too many to count.

6. Those who were called by God "Not My People," would be called "My People."

7. The two kingdoms of Judah and Israel would have one head.

8. Hosea bought back his wife.

9. God's people would call him "My Husband."

10. God would remove the names of the Baals from the mouths of his people.

11. God would betroth Israel to himself forever.

12. The Lord their God.

13. David their king.

14. Come in fear to the Lord and to his goodness.

15. This would occur in "the latter days."

16. Israel's sins from 4:1–2: no faithfulness, steadfast love, or knowledge of God; swearing, lying, murder, stealing, committing adultery, and bloodshed.

17. A morning cloud.

18. Dew that goes away early.

19. The people had made kings.

20. The people had made idols.

21. Calf at Samaria.

22. The people relied on palaces, fortified cities, and strongholds for safety, instead of on God.

23. Lack of knowledge.

24. Hosea called on the people to repent and to press on to know the Lord.

25. Knowledge of God to sacrifices and offerings.

26. Death.

27. Plagues.

28. Sheol.

29. Sting.

30. Compassion.

31. God began to hate his people at Gilgal.

32. God would drive Israel out of his house.

33. God would no longer love them.

34. A moth.

35. Dry rot.

36. A lion.

37. Wild beast.

38. The people would be like morning mist, dew that goes away early, chaff from the threshing floor, and smoke from a window.

39. Father.

40. Child.

41. Walk.

42. Feed.

43. Recoiled.

44. Burning anger.

45. God promised to heal his people's apostasy.

46. To love them freely.

47. Anger has turned away.

Jonah

Jonah 1–4

Jonah 1–4

1. In chapter 1, the wind and sea, the lots, the sailors, the wind and sea again, and the fish all did God's will; the people of Nineveh and Jonah did not do God's will.

2. Overboard.

3. The Lord.

4. Sacrifices.

5. Feared.

6. "Salvation belongs to the LORD!"

7. The sailors said, "You, O LORD, have done as it pleased you."

8. In chapter 2, Jonah did God's will (he prayed); the fish did God's will.

9. In chapter 3, Jonah and the king and people of Nineveh did God's will.

10. Gracious.

11. Merciful.

12. Anger.

13. Steadfast love.

14. Relenting.

15. Die.

16. In chapter 4, the plant, the worm, the scorching east wind, and the sun obeyed God.

17. Question.

Kings and Chronicles: Part 4

2 Kings 15–17

2 Kings
15–17

1. Zechariah; six months; assassinated; did what was evil.

2. Shallum; one month; assassinated; doesn't say—maybe didn't live long enough to be evaluated!

3. Menahem; 10 years; died of natural causes; evil, brutal, violent.

4. Pekahiah; two years; assassinated; did what was evil.

5. Pekah; twenty years; assassinated; did what was evil.

6. Hoshea; nine years; the king of Assyria bound and imprisoned him; evil, but not as bad as other kings.

7. Assyria besieged Samaria for three years.

8. The Israelites were taken away into captivity in Assyria and other places.

9. This occurred because the people of Israel had sinned against the Lord.

10. The Israelites had walked in the customs of the nations God had driven out.

11. They had built high places.

12. They had set up pillars and asherim.

13. They had served idols.

14. God had sent prophets to warn them.

15. The Israelites had not listened to the prophets.

16. Israel had despised God's statutes (laws) and covenant.

17. They had abandoned God's commandments.

18. The Israelites had made and worshiped calves, all the host of heaven, and Baal.

19. They had burned their children as offerings.

20. The Israelites had used divination and omens (black magic).

21. God became very angry and removed them out of his sight.

Test 9
More Kings and More Prophets

Short answer.

1. Israel.   3. Israel.   5. Judah.   7. Judah.

2. Judah.   4. Judah.   6. Nineveh.

Matching.

8. D or G	13. A	18. E	23. E
9. C	14. D	19. D	24. A
10. F	15. A	20. G	25. E
11. D	16. F	21. C	26. F
12. E	17. B	22. B	

Short answer.

27. Three of five kings were assassinated.

28. None of Israel's kings were faithful to God.

29. Assyria besieged Samaria.

30. The Israelites were taken as captives to Assyria and resettled in other cities.

31. The term for God's day of blessing on his people, judgment on his enemies is "the day of the Lord."

32. The near fulfillment of the day of the Lord would be the captivity of the Israelites, followed by their return to the land later.

33. The greater, further off fulfillment of the day of the Lord would be the coming of Christ, with the final, fullest fulfillment when he will come again.

34. The prophet's writings include hope.

35. God can judge sin as it deserves *and* not judge his sinful people because he punished the sin of his people fully in Christ, when he died on the cross. Therefore, God's people can be forgiven and not receive God's wrath and punishment.

Kings and Chronicles: Part 5

2 Chronicles 27–32; 2 Kings 18–20

2 Chronicles 27–32; 2 Kings 18–20

1. Uzziah's son, who became the next king of Judah, was Jotham.

2. He reigned 16 years.

3. Jotham did what was right in the eyes of the Lord.

4. Jotham became mighty.

5. The people still followed corrupt practices.

6. Ahaz followed the ways of kings of Israel; he built Baal images; he burned his sons as offerings.

7. Syria.

8. Assyria.

9. Ahaz became even more faithless.

10. Ahaz cut in pieces the vessels from the temple and shut the doors of the temple.

11. Hezekiah did what was right in the eyes of the Lord, like David; he removed high places, pillars, and idols; he trusted in the Lord and held fast to him; he kept God's commandments.

12. Sennacherib said that the gods of all the other nations had not been able to save those nations from him, so neither could the God of Jerusalem save Jerusalem.

13. Hezekiah wanted all the kingdoms of the earth to know that the Lord alone was God.

14. God rebuked Sennacherib for mocking God and for his arrogance.

15. God had planned Assyria's conquests from long ago.

16. God promised to put his hook in the king's nose and to turn him back by the way he had come.

17. The Lord promised that the Assyrians would not come into the city or shoot an arrow against it, or come before it with a shield, or cast up a siege mound against it.

18. In one night, the angel of the Lord killed 185,000 Assyrian soldiers while they slept.

19. Sennacherib's sons killed him while he worshiped in the temple of his god.

20. Hezekiah wept and prayed.

21. God answered Hezekiah's prayer and offered a sign to prove he would recover.

22. Hezekiah asked that the shadow from the sundial would turn back ten steps, which happened.

Micah

Micah 1–7

Micah 1–7

1. Micah called his message "the word of the LORD that came to Micah."

2. Samaria.

3. Jerusalem.

4. Each section begins with the word "hear."

5. Planning wickedness.

6. Taking from others what is coveted.

7. Not wanting to listen to preaching unless it made the hearers happy.

8. God said he would send disaster.

9. God promised to gather his people together into one flock with their king to lead them, the Lord at their head.

10. The second section was addressed to the heads and rulers of the people.

11. God denounced these sins: The leaders hated good and loved evil; they "ate" the people they were to lead; they perverted justice; they built cities with iniquity and bloodshed; the judges, priests, and prophets accepted bribes and claimed God was on their side.

12. Judgments God would send: The people would pray and God wouldn't answer; there would be no word or guidance from the Lord; Jerusalem would become a heap of ruins and like a plowed field.

13. Blessings God promised: God would be exalted and people from all nations would flock, willingly, to worship and know him; the law and word of the Lord would go out to all nations; there would be no more war and people would dwell in peace.

14. These things would happen in the latter days.

15. Micah's readers could know these things would happen because the mouth of the Lord had spoken.

16. A ruler would come from Bethlehem.

17. His coming forth was from of old, from ancient days.

18. This person would shepherd God's flock in God's strength.

19. His greatness would extend to the ends of the earth.

20. He would be his people's peace.

21. This person is the Messiah, the Lord Jesus Christ.

22. In the third section, God spoke against his people.

23. God complained against the sins of dishonest business practices, violence, and lying.

24. As punishment, God would strike his people and make them desolate.

25. The boundaries of the people of God would be greatly extended.

26. People from Egypt and Assyria would come to join God's people.

27. People from the nations would come trembling and in great dread, turning to the Lord.

28. There is no God like God; he pardons iniquity; he doesn't keep his anger forever; he delights in steadfast love.

29. God has compassion on his people; he removes their sins.

30. God shows faithfulness and steadfast love to his people; he keeps his covenant promises.

Isaiah

Isaiah 1–39

1. Isaiah saw the Lord high, lifted up, on a throne, and with the train of his robe filling the temple.

2. The seraphim covered their faces with one set of wings and covered their feet with the other set.

3. Holy, holy, holy.

4. The seraphim said that the earth is full of God's glory.

5. Isaiah's first reaction was to cry, "Woe is me!" because of his, and his people's, guilt.

6. The seraph took a coal from the altar.

7. The seraph touched the coal to Isaiah's lips.

8. He told Isaiah his guilt had been taken away and his sin had been atoned for.

9. Isaiah said, "Here am I! Send me."

10. Dull.

11. Heavy.

12. Blind.

13. See.

14. Hear.

15. Understand.

16. Turn and be healed.

17. Verses 1–5 refer to the latter days.

18. The mountain of the house of the Lord would be established as highest of the mountains.

19. Many peoples would come to it.

20. They would come to learn God's ways and walk in his paths.

21. God's law would go out of Zion.

22. God's word would go out of Jerusalem.

23. Men would hide from the terror of the Lord, the splendor of his majesty.

24. Men's pride would be brought low; the Lord alone would be exalted.

25. This would be in that day; on the day the Lord of hosts would have.

26. Men would throw away their idols, to better flee the terror of the Lord.

27. Farmer/vine grower.

28. Vineyard.

29. Bloodshed.

30. Justice.

31. An outcry.

32. Righteousness.

33. Trampled.

34. Waste.

35. Greed that oppressed the poor.

36. Living for pleasure and forgetting the Lord.

37. Sinning largely and freely, and mocking God while sinning.

38. Calling evil good and good evil.

39. Being wise in one's own eyes.

40. Drunkenness or overindulgence.

41. Injustice.

42. God's sinful people before God's wrath would be like dry grass before flame.

43. The law of God.

44. The word of the Holy One of Israel.

45. Anger.

46. Whistle.

47. Come.

48. Distress, darkness, and the gloom of anguish.

49. Gloom.

50. Anguish.

51. Darkness.

52. Light.

53. This would be in the latter time.

54. Galilee of the nations (or Gentiles) would be made glorious.

55. To us a child is born—reminds us of God's promise to Eve that the seed of the woman would crush the Serpent's head.

56. God's promise to David, that a descendant of his would rule forever.

57. Child.

58. Son.

59. Mighty God.

60. Prince of Peace.

61. Never end.

62. Isaiah's hearers could know this would happen because the zeal of the Lord of hosts would do it.

63. Rod.

64. Anger.

65. God had sent Assyria.

66. A godless nation (Israel).

67. Destroy.

68. Assyria's sin and mistake was in thinking that God was like the idols of the other nations.

69. Adjectives used to describe the king of Assyria are "boastful" and "arrogant."

70. God would punish him when God had finished his work on Jerusalem.

71. Assyria.

72. The one who hews with the axe and wields the saw was God.

73. God said he would send a wasting sickness on the Assyrian warriors.

74. The prophecy was against the king of Babylon.

75. God condemned him for his arrogance.

76. Isaiah prophesied against Assyria.

77. Philistia.

78. Moab.

79. Damascus (capital of Syria).

80. Cush.

81. Egypt.

82. Tyre and Sidon.

83. The whole earth.

84. The earth's inhabitants defile it.

85. They have transgressed the laws, violated the statutes, and broken the everlasting covenant.

86. Terror, the pit, the snare will come upon the inhabitants of the earth.

87. The Lord will punish the host of heaven and the kings of the earth.

88. This will occur "on that day."

89. We know because the Lord has spoken this word.

90. The Lord will make a feast for all peoples (for people from all the nations).

91. He will swallow up death forever.

92. He will wipe away all tears.

93. This will occur "on that day."

94. We know these things will happen, for the mouth of the Lord has spoken.

Isaiah 40–66

Isaiah 40–66

1. The "voice crying in the wilderness" was John the Baptist.

2. The glory of the Lord would be revealed.

3. All flesh would see it.

4. People would know this would happen because the mouth of the Lord had spoken it.

5. People were compared to grass and flowers.

6. Grass and flowers exist for only a short time, and people's lives are short (compared to eternity).

7. The word of the Lord is contrasted with grass; the word of the Lord stands forever.

8. The Lord God's coming is announced.

9. His reward would be with him.

10. He would shepherd his flock.

11. Gently.

12. God measures all those waters in the hollow of his hand.

13. God marks off the heavens with a span.

14. God is able to measure all the dust of the planet.

15. God weighs the mountains in a scale.

16. No one advised or taught God.

17. Nothing can be compared to God; nothing and no one is like him.

18. God asks, "To whom then will you compare me, that I should be like him?"

19. Hidden.

20. Weary.

21. Understanding.

22. God will provide power and renewed strength to those who wait for the Lord.

23. God says he can tell what's going to happen, then cause it to happen, while idols cannot.

24. An important difference between God and idols is that God lives and can do things, while idols are not alive and can do nothing.

25. Spirit.

26. The nations.

27. No.

28. No.

29. Covenant.

30. The people.

31. Light.

32. Nations.

33. God will not give *his glory* to anyone else.

34. God proves he is God by telling what will happen before it happens.

35. Five times, God said there was no God but him. ("Besides me there is no god; Who is like me? Is there a God besides me? There is no Rock; I know not any.")

36. The idol worshiper uses half of the wood for his fire.

37. He uses the other half to make a god that he worships, asking it to save him.

38. Knowledge.

39. Discernment.

40. Forgives sin; redeems his people.

41. Forms people inside their mothers; created the universe and the earth.

42. Frustrates men's plans.

43. Brings to pass what his prophets said would happen.

44. "Rebuilt and inhabited."

45. Be laid.

46. "Fulfill all my purpose."

47. God would subdue nations and kings before Cyrus and open doors before him and give him treasures.

48. God would do these things for the sake of his people, Israel.

49. God intended all this to show to all people that there is no God but God.

50. God also forms light *and* creates darkness; he makes well-being *and* creates calamity.

51. Five. (Isaiah 45:14–25 says there is no God but God in verse 14, verse 18, twice in verse 21, verse 22; verse 24 makes a similar statement).

52. Verse 21.

53. God called all the ends of the earth to turn to him and be saved.

54. Every knee would bow and every tongue would swear allegiance.

55. We know this will happen because the word has gone forth from God's mouth and won't return.

56. God swore by himself.

57. Beasts and livestock carried the Babylonian gods.

58. The idols could not even save themselves, let alone anyone else.

59. God carried his people, from birth to old age.

60. God would also save his people.

61. God said he is the only God, and no one is like him.

62. Stand.

63. All his purpose.

64. He was wounded for our transgressions.

65. He was crushed for our iniquities.

66. His chastisement brought our peace.

67. We have all gone astray and turned to our own way.

68. God laid our iniquity on him.

69. By his offering for sin, the will of the Lord prospered in his hand; he made many to be accounted righteous/justified the many.

70. Redeemer.

71. Spirit.

72. Words.

73. Children.

74. Any nation that wouldn't serve the people of God would perish and be laid to waste.

75. Savior.

76. Redeemer.

77. Violence and destruction; the sun and moon; mourning would be no more.

78. The LORD.

79. I will hasten it.

80. Jesus said he was the fulfillment of this prophecy.

81. Clothing.

82. A robe.

83. God would create new heavens and a new earth.

84. God would rejoice and be glad in Jerusalem and his people.

85. God would gather all the nations.

86. They would see his glory.

87. Then they would declare his glory among the nations.

88. The brothers of the people of God would be brought from all the nations.

89. God would make of some of them priests and Levites.

90. All flesh would come to worship before the Lord.

91. The future of those who rebelled against God would be the worm that shall not die and the fire that shall not be quenched; they would be abhorrent to all.

Joel 1–3

Joel 1–3

1. Locusts.

2. Drunkards.

3. The wine and vines, fig trees, grain, oil (from olives), wheat, barley, pomegranates, palms, and apples had all been damaged or destroyed.

4. Cattle.

5. Sheep.

6. Beasts of the field, the wild animals.

7. Priests.

8. Cry out.

9. Day of the Lord.

10. Near.

11. Destruction from the Almighty.

12. Before, the land was like the garden of Eden.

13. After, the land was a desolate wilderness.

14. It was the Lord's army.

15. Words describing the day of the Lord: coming; near; darkness; gloom; clouds and thick darkness; great; very awesome; who can endure it?

16. God called his people to return to him.

17. God told them, "Rend your hearts and not your garments."

18. Gracious.

19. Merciful.

20. Slow to anger.

21. Abounding in steadfast love.

22. Relents.

23. God would remove the enemy (the northerner) from the midst of his people.

24. Israel would know that God was in their midst, and that he was their God and there is no other.

25. God promised to pour out his Spirit on all kinds of people.

26. This would be when the day of the Lord came.

27. "And it shall come to pass that everyone who calls on the name of the LORD shall be saved."

28. Days.

29. Time.

30. Nations.

31. Judgment.

32. His people.

33. Roar.

34. Refuge.

35. Stronghold.

Kings and Chronicles: Part 6

2 Kings 21–25; 2 Chronicles 33–36

2 Kings 21–25; 2 Chronicles 33–36

1. Manasseh was twelve years old when he became king of Judah.

2. He built altars for all the host of heaven; he put the altars in the two courts of the house of the Lord.

3. He burnt his son as an offering.

4. Manasseh used fortune telling and omens.

5. He put the carved image of Asherah in the house of the Lord.

6. Manasseh led the people into more evil than the nations whom the Lord had destroyed from the land had done.

7. Manasseh also shed much innocent blood.

8. The next king was Amon.

9. Yes, he was like his father.

10. He reigned two years.

11. Amon was killed by his subjects.

12. Josiah became king after Amon.

13. He was eight years old.

14. Josiah did what was right; he walked in the way of David; he did not turn aside to the right or the left.

15. When he was twelve, Josiah began to purge Jerusalem of high places, altars, and idols.

16. When he was twenty-six, he began to repair the house of the Lord.

17. The Book of the Law of the Lord was found in the temple.

18. Josiah tore his clothes.

19. He knew God's wrath must be great against the Jews because they had not kept what was in the book.

20. The prophetess said God would bring disaster upon Judah because of the people's sin.

21. This would not happen until after Josiah's lifetime, because Josiah had humbled himself and wept when he had heard God's Word.

22. Josiah had the book read to all the people.

23. The book is called the Book of the Covenant.

24. Josiah celebrated the Passover.

25. People from the kingdom of Judah *and* people from Israel were there.

26. Josiah died in battle.

27. All the people mourned at Josiah's death.

28. Jeremiah wrote a lament for Josiah.

Zephaniah

Zephaniah 1–3

Zephaniah 1–3

1. Josiah.

2. Judah.

3. 17.

4. All the earth.

5. Judah and Jerusalem.

6. Baal.

7. Priests.

8. Idols.

9. The Lord would search diligently for those who were complacent, saying God wouldn't do anything; when he found them, he would punish them.

10. Great; near; hastening fast; bitter; wrath; distress; anguish; ruin; devastation; darkness; gloom; clouds and thick darkness; trumpet blast and battle cry.

11. Shameless.

12. Make their deeds corrupt.

13. Philistines.

14. Moab.

15. Ammonites.

16. Cushites.

17. Assyria.

18. Nineveh.

19. Nineveh said, "I am, and there is no one else."

20. Rebellious.

21. Defiled.

22. Correction.

23. In the Lord.

24. Draw near.

25. Prophets.

26. Priests.

27. Call upon the name of the Lord.

28. Serve.

29. God's worshipers would come from beyond Cush.

30. In that day, God's people would be humble, seeking refuge in the name of the Lord, just, truthful, and unafraid.

31. God called his people to rejoice that God had taken away his judgments and their enemies, and their King was in their midst, so they would never need to fear evil.

32. God would rejoice over his people.

Obadiah

Obadiah

Obadiah

1. This prophecy is about the nation of Edom.

2. Violence.

3. Stood aloof.

4. One of them.

5. Gloated over.

6. Looted.

7. Cut off.

8. Handed over.

9. Pride.

10. Nest.

11. Stars.

12. Bring them down.

13. All nations.

14. Of the Lord.

15. Stubble.

16. Fire.

17. Saviors.

18. Mount Esau.

19. The Lord's.

Nahum

Nahum 1–3

Nahum 1–3

1. Jealous; avenging; wrathful; taking vengeance on his adversaries; keeping wrath for his enemies; slow to anger yet great in power and by no means clearing the guilty; none can stand before his indignation or endure the heat of his anger; he pours out wrath like fire and breaks rocks in pieces.

2. The Lord knows those who take refuge in him.

3. The Lord is good.

4. A stronghold in the day of trouble.

5. The Lord will make a complete end of his adversaries.

6. Pursue them into darkness.

7. Nineveh.

8. Judah.

9. Nineveh.

10. Judah.

11. God promised to restore his people's majesty.

12. Idolatry.

13. Bloodshed.

14. Lies.

15. Prostitute.

Habakkuk

Habakkuk 1–3

Habakkuk 1–3

1. God did not hear Habakkuk's cry or save.

2. God looked at wrong idly.

3. The wicked surrounded the righteous.

4. God would raise up the Babylonians.

5. These people were bitter, hasty, dreaded, and fearsome.

6. These people seized dwellings that didn't belong to them as they marched along.

7. They were fiercer than evening wolves.

8. They came for violence.

9. They gathered captives like sand.

10. Their own might was their god.

11. God is everlasting, holy, a Rock, too pure to look at evil or wrong.

12. Ordained.

13. Judgment.

14. The wicked swallowed up the man more righteous than he.

15. The fish or like crawling things.

16. Ruler.

17. Heaps up what is not his own.

18. Gets evil gain for his house.

19. Builds a town with blood.

20. Makes his neighbors drink.

21. Worships idols.

22. The earth will be filled with the knowledge of the glory of the Lord.

23. As fully as the waters cover the sea.

24. The vision awaits its appointed time.

25. Come.

26. The righteous shall live by his faith.

27. His holy temple.

28. Silence.

29. Mercy.

30. Habakkuk was frightened; we know it because of his trembling body and legs, his quivering lips, and the feeling of rottenness in his bones.

31. Habakkuk chose to rejoice in the Lord.

32. Strength.

Test 10
Hope for a Glorious Future

Matching.

1. M	**7.** J	**13.** I	**19.** I
2. J	**8.** I	**14.** I	**20.** H
3. H	**9.** M	**15.** J	**21.** I
4. M	**10.** Z	**16.** I	**22.** O
5. J	**11.** J	**17.** O	**23.** Z
6. H	**12.** H	**18.** N	

Short essay.

24. The prophets wrote, first, of the sins of God's people, which would explain why the terrible events of the captivity were happening to them, and why God was no longer giving them victory and protecting them. The prophets also wrote of the future, assuring God's people that God had not finished working out his plans, but would restore them, destroy their (and God's) enemies, and give his people a glorious future.

Jeremiah and Lamentations

Jeremiah 1–29

Jeremiah 1–29

1. God appointed Jeremiah to be a prophet before he was born.

2. God would be with Jeremiah to deliver him.

3. God put his words into Jeremiah's mouth.

4. Jeremiah would be over nations to pluck up and break down, to destroy them and overthrow, and to build and plant.

5. God was watching over his word to perform it.

6. Wound.

7. The sins of the people included: adultery, treachery, falsehood, proceeding from evil to evil, and not knowing the Lord.

8. The people should not boast in wisdom, might, or riches.

9. They should boast in understanding and knowing the Lord.

10. Pashhur, the priest, had Jeremiah beaten and put in the stocks.

11. Deceived.

12. Mocked.

13. A reproach and derision.

14. Hold in.

15. His fall.

16. Dread warrior.

17. Overcome.

18. Day he was born.

19. The prophets and priests were ungodly.

20. The false prophets got their visions from their own minds.

21. Sent.

22. Spoken.

23. Their message would have been: "Turn from your evil way; repent."

24. Straw.

25. Wheat.

26. God said he was against those who claimed to speak his word but didn't.

27. Do all the prophet's predictions come true?

28. The false prophets said to those who despised the word of the Lord, "It shall be well with you; no disaster shall come upon you."

29. Yes.

30. The prophet preached rebellion.

31. Does the prophet obey God and teach others to do the same?

32. The false prophets were committing adultery, walking in lies, and strengthening the hands of the evildoers.

33. Teaching.

34. Testimony.

35. God's curse is for such people; peace and safety is for those who are faithful to his covenant.

Jeremiah 30–52

Jeremiah 30–52

1. The king cut off that piece with his knife and threw it in the fire.

2. The king and his servants were not afraid, and they were not repentant.

3. God gave the message to Jeremiah again, to dictate as Baruch—his secretary—wrote it down.

4. Jeremiah was arrested for "deserting to the Chaldeans."

5. Jeremiah was put in the dungeon cells.

6. Jeremiah was arrested for discouraging people by telling them to surrender to the Babylonians, as God wanted them to do.

7. Jeremiah was put into an unused cistern with mud into which he sank; he would have died of hunger without Ebed-melech's intervention.

8. The Babylonians had besieged Jerusalem so that there was no food inside.

9. The king tried to escape through a hole in the city wall.

10. The Babylonians killed his sons before him, put out his eyes, and took him as a prisoner to Babylon.

11. The temple's valuables were carried off to Babylon and the temple was burned.

12. Only the poorest of the poor remained in Jerusalem.

Lamentations 1–5

Lamentations 1–5

1. The Lord's steadfast love and mercies never cease or end.

2. The Lord's faithfulness is great.

3. The Lord is the writer's portion.

4. Cast off.

5. Forever.

6. Compassion.

7. "Should we go to Egypt, or not?"

8. The people promised to do whatever God told Jeremiah to tell them.

9. Jeremiah's answer from the Lord was, "Don't go to Egypt."

10. The people's response was, "You're lying; we're going anyway."

11. The people forced Jeremiah to go along with them to Egypt.

12. God's promises in 29:10-14: God would bring the Jews back to their land after 70 years; he would give them a future and a hope; they would call on him and he would hear them; they would seek him with a whole heart and find him; he would restore their fortunes; he would gather them from the nations where they'd been scattered.

13. God promised to make a new covenant.

14. God would put his law inside his people and write it on their hearts.

15. God.

16. People.

17. God would forgive his people's sin and not remember it.

18. God would surely keep this covenant forever and would never cast off his people.

19. Then Judah would be saved.

20. The name is "the LORD is our righteousness."

21. David.

22. The Levitical priests.

23. Abraham, Isaac, and Jacob in 33:26.

Ezekiel

Ezekiel 1–32

1. Ezekiel was beside the Chebar canal among the exiles.

2. The cloud coming from the north was bright, flashing fire, and had, as it were, gleaming metal in the middle.

3. There were four creatures.

4. The creatures had four faces: faces of a man, a lion, an ox, and an eagle.

5. Two wings covered their bodies and two wings touched the others creatures' wings.

6. The legs were straight with calf-like feet that sparkled like burnished bronze.

7. The overall appearance of the creatures was like burning coals or torches.

8. The creatures darted to and fro like lightning.

9. Beside each creature was a wheel with a wheel inside of it, with eyes all around the rims.

10. Above the expanse was something like a throne, like sapphire.

11. The one on the throne glowed like gleaming metal above the waist and burned like fire below it.

12. All around the one on the throne was brightness like a bright rainbow.

13. The glory of the LORD.

14. God gave Ezekiel a scroll with writing on it; Ezekiel was to eat it.

15. Ezekiel sat by the Chebar canal overwhelmed for seven days.

16. "I am the LORD; I have spoken."

17. " . . . and you shall know that I am the LORD."

18. Ezekiel was taken to Jerusalem.

19. Ezekiel saw the glory of the Lord.

20. The idolatry and evil were happening in the house of the Lord.

21. The threshold of the house (temple).

22. The east gate.

23. These evildoers would know that God was the Lord.

24. God promised to bring his people back from the countries where he had scattered them and give them the land of Israel again.

25. Spirit.

26. Heart of stone.

27. Heart of flesh.

28. Walk in his statues and keep his rules and obey them

29. His people.

30. Their God.

31. The glory of the Lord left the city and went out to the mountain.

32. The Ammonites.

33. Moab.

34. Edom.

35. The Philistines.

36. Tyre.

37. Sidon.

38. Egypt.

39. That I am the LORD.

Ezekiel 33–48

Ezekiel 33–48

1. Watchman.

2. Warn of impending disaster.

3. The blood of those who died.

4. God takes no pleasure in the death of the wicked.

5. Will you die?

6. Jerusalem had fallen.

7. The reason God would act was not for Israel's sake; the reason was for the sake of his holy name.

8. The nations would know that God was the Lord.

9. God would cleanse his people of all their uncleanness and idols.

10. God would give them a new heart and a new spirit, a heart of flesh in place of their heart of stone.

11. God would put his own Spirit in them and cause them to walk in his statutes and obey his rules.

12. The heart of the covenant: "You shall be my people, and I will be your God."

13. They would know that God was the Lord.

14. The valley was full of bones that were very dry.

15. God asked, "Can these bones live?"

16. God told Ezekiel to prophesy to the bones.

17. Ezekiel was to tell the bones to hear the word of the Lord.

18. The bones would know that God is the Lord.

19. The rattling noise was the sound of bones coming together and reconnecting.

20. Breath was still missing.

21. Breath entered the bones and they lived.

22. The bones represented the house of Israel.

23. Graves.

24. Spirit.

25. Live.

26. Their land.

27. God was the Lord.

28. God said, "I have spoken, and I will do it."

29. Ezekiel saw the glory of the Lord come from the east, enter the temple, and fill it.

30. God said he would dwell in the midst of his people forever.

31. Water.

32. Trickle.

33. Ankle-deep.

34. Waist-deep.

35. Impassable.

36. Swim in.

37. The sea.

38. Every living creature.

39. Trees.

40. Wither.

41. Fail.

42. Healing.

43. In Revelation 22, there is a river of life flowing from God's presence—in Revelation, from a throne, in Ezekiel from a temple. There are trees on both sides of the river, with twelve kinds of fruit, year round, and the leaves are for the healing of the nations.

Daniel 1–6

1. The men were to be educated for three years, then serve the king.

2. Daniel did not want to eat the king's food.

3. Daniel asked to be fed for ten days on vegetables and water; then he and his friends should be compared with the other young men to see if they appeared to be as healthy.

4. Tell the king what the dream was.

5. The king wanted to be sure the magicians really had the ability to tell the meaning.

6. Daniel praised God.

7. Removes.

8. Sets up.

9. Reveals.

10. Hidden.

11. The statue was made of gold, then silver, then bronze, then iron and iron mixed with clay.

12. A stone cut without hands knocked the statue down and its pieces blew away.

13. The stone represented a kingdom God would set up which would never be destroyed.

14. The stone became a great mountain and filled the whole earth.

15. Shadrach, Meshach, and Abednego refused to worship the king's image.

16. No; they said God was able to deliver them, but even if he didn't, they would not worship the king's image.

17. The king saw three unburned young men, loose and walking around, plus a fourth man.

18. Delivered.

19. Trusted.

20. Spoke against this God.

21. Torn limb from limb.

22. Laid in ruins.

23. No other god.

24. Nebuchadnezzar wrote chapter 4.

25. An everlasting kingdom.

26. Endures from generation to generation.

27. Tree.

28. Ends of the earth.

29. Heaven.

30. Chop down.

31. Stump.

32. Dew.

33. Beast's.

34. Seven.

35. Most High.

36. Kingdom of men.

37. Whom he will.

38. King Nebuchadnezzar.

39. Animals.

40. Grass.

41. Power.

42. Majesty.

43. Grass.

44. Eagles' feathers.

45. Birds' claws.

46. His will.

47. Stay his hand.

48. God is called the Most High.

49. God is also called King of heaven.

50. Belshazzar used vessels taken from the temple.

51. Belshazzar praised idols.

52. He saw a man's hand, writing on the wall.

53. Was lifted up.

54. Hardened.

55. Proudly.

56. Kingdom of mankind.

57. Whom he wills.

58. Humbled his heart.

59. Lord of heaven.

60. Honored.

61. Breath.

62. An end.

63. Wanting.

64. Divided.

65. Medes.

66. Persians.

67. Killed.

68. Darius the Mede.

69. The king planned to set Daniel over the whole kingdom.

70. Concerning the law of his God.

71. The law said that, for thirty days, no one could pray to anyone except the king.

72. Daily, Daniel prayed by the window, facing Jerusalem, three times.

73. Daniel did just as he had done previously.

74. The law had been signed by the king and, according to the law of the Medes and Persians, that meant it could not be changed.

75. The king said, "May your God deliver you."

76. Daniel said God had sent his angel to shut the lions' mouths.

77. When Daniel's enemies and their families were thrown in, the lions caught them and broke all their bones before they even hit the ground.

78. Living God.

79. Kingdom.

80. To the end.

Daniel 7–14

1. The beasts came out of the sea.

2. The first beast was like a lion with eagles' wings.

3. The second beast looked like a bear and it was told to arise and devour flesh.

4. The third beast was like a leopard with four wings on its back and four heads.

5. Terrifying.

6. Dreadful.

7. Exceedingly strong.

8. Its teeth were iron.

9. The fourth beast was killed and its body was destroyed.

10. The one who came was like a son of man.

11. Dominion, glory, and a kingdom were given to him.

12. All peoples, languages, and nations would serve him.

13. Everlasting.

14. Pass away.

15. Be destroyed.

16. Wage war.

17. Prevail.

18. The kingdom and the dominion would be given to the people of the saints of the Most High.

Test 11
The Fall of Jerusalem

Short answer.

1. The weeping prophet.

2. Reasons for Jeremiah's weeping: his message of judgment; his people's sin; the persecution he endured for his message—mockery, beatings, imprisonment; the people's hostility to his message and refusal to repent; the opposition of false prophets; his trip into Egypt against his will.

3. Daniel and Ezekiel.

4. King Jehoiakim cut up the scroll and burned the pieces.

5. King Zedekiah was caught trying to escape; the Babylonians killed his sons in front of him, blinded his eyes, and took him as a prisoner to Babylon.

6. King Nebuchadnezzar lost his man's mind and could no longer rule as king. He lived outside and ate grass like an animal, while his hair grew long and his fingernails grew like claws.

7. Belshazzar saw a hand writing on the wall of his palace. The writing described the coming judgment. That very night, his kingdom was taken and he was killed.

8. The Persian Empire (or the Medes and the Persians) conquered Babylon.

9. Daniel broke the law saying no one could pray to anyone but the king for thirty days.

10. The main point of the book of Daniel is that God rules over all kingdoms. He chooses who will be king and for how long. His kingdom will never end. This was appropriate for the people of God at the time because it looked like a powerful, idolatrous king had been able to conquer the people of God.

11. "And you/they will know that I am the LORD."

12. New covenant promises: God would give his people a new heart; he would put his Spirit in them; he would remove their heart of stone and give them a heart of flesh; his laws would be written on their hearts.

Short essay.

13. Vision of dry bones: found in Ezekiel; many scattered, dried-out bones; at God's command, Ezekiel prophesied to them and they came together; at God's command, Ezekiel prophesied to the breath to enter them, and they came to life. Hopelessly impossible as it seemed, God would restore his people to their land and give them hope. Ultimately, God would put his Spirit into spiritually dead people and give them life at the preaching of his Word.

Nebuchadnezzar's dream of a statue: found in Daniel; a great statue made of gold, silver, bronze, and iron was knocked over by a rock cut without hands. The statue pieces blew away, while the rock grew to be a mountain that filled the whole earth. The Persians would overthrow the Babylonian empire, then be overthrown by the Greeks, who would in turn be overthrown by the Romans. While the Romans ruled, God's kingdom would begin. It would overthrow all kingdoms and grow until it filled the earth and it would never end.

Daniel's dream of beasts: found in Daniel; four beasts came out of the sea. The first was like a lion with eagles' wings (Babylon); the second was like a bear (Persia); the third was like a four-headed leopard with four wings (Greece); and the fourth was a terrifying beast (Rome). One like a son of man came up to the throne where the Ancient of Days sat and received a kingdom that would last forever, while the other kingdoms were destroyed. Even those strong kingdoms that persecute the people of God will be overthrown and the people of God will rule with Christ.

Ezra, Nehemiah, Haggai, and Zechariah

Ezra 1–4

Ezra 1–4

1. Jews should return to Jerusalem and rebuild the house of the Lord.

2. The Lord stirred up Cyrus's spirit to do this, so that the word of the Lord from Jeremiah might be fulfilled.

3. The Jews rebuilt the altar.

4. Jeshua.

5. Zerubbabel.

6. The Jews began to rebuild the temple.

7. The noise was caused by people shouting for joy that this much was accomplished, and by people weeping because they remembered the old temple.

8. The Jews' response was "No."

9. The neighbors discouraged the people from building by making them afraid, and bribed counselors to frustrate their purpose.

Haggai 1–2

Haggai 1–2

1. The Jews' houses were paneled (fairly luxurious), while the Lord's house lay in ruins.

2. The Jews had economic problems and God had withheld the rain from their crops.

3. The Jews obeyed God and Haggai, and feared the Lord.

4. The Lord stirred up their spirits.

5. The new temple was as nothing in their eyes.

6. The treasures of the nations would come in.

7. God promised to fill his temple with glory.

8. The latter glory of the temple would be greater than its former glory.

9. God would give peace.

Zechariah 1–14

Zechariah 1–14

1. First vision: a man on a red horse, and behind him red, sorrel, and white horses.

2. Second vision: four horns and four craftsmen.

3. Third vision: a man with a measuring line.

4. The apple of God's eye.

5. Fourth vision: Joshua in dirty clothes was accused by Satan; the angel of the Lord commanded that his dirty clothes be removed and that he be clothed in clean ones.

6. Fifth vision: a golden lampstand with a bowl, seven lamps, and seven lips, with an olive tree on each side.

7. Might.

8. Power.

9. My Spirit.

10. Sixth vision: a giant flying scroll, with writing on both sides.

11. Seventh vision: a woman inside a basket, with a heavy lid on it, carried away by flying women.

12. Zechariah was to have a crown made and put it on the head of Joshua.

13. A priest would be on the throne.

14. God's king was described as riding into Jerusalem on a donkey colt.

15. This king would speak peace to the nations, and his rule would extend from sea to sea and to the ends of the earth.

16. God promised to pour out on his people a spirit of grace and pleas for mercy.

17. A fountain would be opened for God's people, to cleanse them from sin.

Ezra 5–10

Ezra 5–10

1. Darius required the Jews' adversaries to pay for the rebuilding of the temple and to provide animals for daily sacrifices.

2. The Jews celebrated the Passover.

3. Ezra was a scribe, skilled in the Law of Moses, who had set his heart to study the Law of the Lord, and to do it and to teach it.

4. The people had married people from the other nations.

Nehemiah 1–13

Nehemiah 1–13

1. Nehemiah lived in Susa; he was cupbearer to the king.

2. The walls of Jerusalem were still in ruins.

3. Nehemiah wept, mourned, fasted, and prayed.

4. Keeps covenant and steadfast love with those who love him and keep his commandments.

5. In 1:6b-7, Nehemiah confessed his and the people's sin.

6. Gather his people and bring them back to the place where his name dwelt.

7. People.

8. Servants.

9. Redeemed.

10. Nehemiah asked God to be attentive to his prayers, to give him success, and to grant him mercy.

11. Nehemiah prayed before answering the king.

12. Nehemiah asked that the king send him to Jerusalem to rebuild the walls.

13. Nehemiah said he received what he asked for because "the good hand of [his] God was upon [him]."

14. The enemy neighbors were displeased "that someone had come to seek the welfare of the people of Israel."

15. The Jews in Jerusalem responded by rising up to work.

16. The enemy neighbors jeered at them and accused them of rebellion against the king.

17. The high priest and his brothers.

18. Goldsmiths.

19. Perfumers.

20. Merchants.

21. Ruler.

22. His house.

23. Daughters.

24. The Dung Gate.

25. Stoop.

26. Nehemiah prayed when Sanballat jeered at the Jews.

27. The wall quickly reached half its height because the people had a mind to work.

28. Sanballat.

29. Tobiah.

30. Arabs.

31. Ammonites.

32. Ashdodites.

33. The angry enemies were going to fight against Jerusalem.

34. Nehemiah and the people prayed, and set a guard as protection.

35. Construction.

36. Weapons.

37. The break of dawn.

38. The stars came out.

39. The enemies intended to do harm to Nehemiah.

40. They said Nehemiah was rebuilding the wall because the Jews intended to rebel and he wished to be their king.

41. Nehemiah responded to the enemies' accusation by praying for God to strengthen him.

42. The enemies wanted Nehemiah to be afraid and to sin, to give him a bad name.

43. Nehemiah responded by praying.

44. It had taken only 52 days to complete the wall.

45. The enemies and neighbors were afraid and fell greatly in their own esteem.

46. These people realized that the work had been accomplished with the help of God.

47. Ezra read the book of the Law of Moses from early morning until midday.

48. For a quarter of the day, the people read from the book of the Law.

49. For another quarter of the day, they confessed their sins.

50. Making everything.

51. Abraham.

52. Egypt.

53. Divided the sea.

54. Led.

55. Right rules and true laws.

56. Bread.

57. Water.

58. The next part of the prayer describes the people's sin and unfaithfulness, and how God had finally given them to their enemies.

59. Covenant.

Esther

Esther 1–10

Esther 1–10

1. 180 days.

2. The purpose of the party was for the king to display his riches, splendor, and the pomp of his greatness.

3. The king's wife wouldn't come when he ordered her to come.

4. Vashti was removed from being queen.

5. The king's letter decreed that every man must be master in his own household.

6. The plan was to gather beautiful, young virgins from all over the empire from among whom the king would choose the one he liked to be the next queen.

7. Esther was Mordecai's orphaned cousin, whom he was raising.

8. Esther had a beautiful figure and was lovely to look at.

9. Esther pleased the man in charge of the young women and won his favor.

10. The king loved Esther more than all the women.

11. Mordecai overheard a plot to kill the king.

12. The incident was recorded in the book of the chronicles of the king.

13. Haman.

14. Agagite.

15. Mordecai wouldn't bow to Haman.

16. Haman decided to destroy Mordecai and his entire nation.

17. Haman chose the day by casting lots.

18. The word for lots was "Pur."

19. Destroy.

20. Kill.

21. Annihilate.

22. Jews.

23. Young.

24. Old.

25. Women.

26. Children.

27. One.

28. Mordecai wanted Esther to go to the king and plead for her people.

29. Esther didn't want to go to the king because doing so uninvited meant death—unless the king happened to hold out his scepter.

30. Esther said, "And if I perish, I perish."

31. Esther won favor in the sight of the king, and he held out the scepter to her.

32. Esther asked the king and Haman to come to a feast she would prepare.

33. At the feast, Esther asked for the king and Haman to come to another feast.

34. Haman's good mood was ruined by seeing Mordecai, who still did not bow to him.

35. Haman built a gallows to hang Mordecai on.

36. The king couldn't sleep.

37. The king gave orders to have the book of memorable deeds, the chronicles, read to him.

38. The story that was read to the king was the one about Mordecai saving the king's life.

39. Haman walked in.

40. Haman came up with so many great ideas because he thought he was the one whom the king wanted to honor.

41. Haman had to publicly honor Mordecai.

42. The king left the room because he was angry.

43. The king found Haman on the queen's couch.

44. The king thought that Haman was assaulting the queen.

45. Haman was hanged on the gallows he had prepared for Mordecai.

46. Gain the mastery.

47. Reverse.

48. Mordecai.

49. Jews.

50. Fear of the Jews.

51. Sorrow.

52. Gladness.

53. Mourning.

54. Holiday.

Malachi

Malachi 1–4

1. Loved.
2. Loved.
3. Loved.
4. Hated.
5. Despised.
6. Polluted food.
7. Altar.
8. Blind animals.
9. Lame or sick.
10. Governor.
11. Great.
12. The nations.
13. Weariness.
14. Feared.
15. A foreign god.
16. Faithless.
17. Wearied.
18. Words.
19. Wearied.
20. Delights.
21. Justice.
22. The Lord.
23. The covenant.
24. Purify.
25. Fire.
26. Soap.
27. Judgment.
28. Turned aside.
29. Change.
30. Rob.
31. Robbing.
32. Robbed.
33. Tithes and contributions.
34. Hard.
35. Serve God.
36. Evildoers.
37. Remembrance.
38. Fear.
39. Esteem.
40. Treasured.
41. Ablaze.
42. Stubble.
43. Sun of righteousness.
44. Healing.
45. Law.
46. Elijah.
47. Hearts of fathers.
48. Children.
49. Hearts of the children.
50. Fathers.
51. Decree of utter destruction.

Test 12
The Old Testament Books (excluding Poetry Books)

Identify.

1. 1–2 Chronicles.
2. Judges.
3. Daniel.
4. 1–2 Kings.
5. Deuteronomy.
6. Lamentations.
7. Esther.
8. Leviticus.
9. Exodus.
10. Malachi.
11. Ezekiel.

12. Micah.
13. Ezra.
14. Nahum.
15. Genesis.
16. Nehemiah.
17. Numbers.
18. Habakkuk.
19. Obadiah.
20. Haggai.
21. Ruth.
22. Hosea.

23. Isaiah.
24. 1–2 Samuel.
25. Jeremiah.
26. Zechariah.
27. Joel.
28. Jonah.
29. Joshua.
30. Zephaniah.
31. Amos.

Hebrew Poetry

Hebrew Poetry

Hebrew Poetry

1. The two lines of Proverbs 9:9 say basically the same thing in different ways.

2. The point of Proverbs 9:9 is that a wise person receives instruction and becomes even wiser.

3. The main point of Proverbs 9:10 is that a right attitude toward God is the most important thing in becoming wise.

4. The main point of Proverbs 9:11 is that exercising wisdom results in a longer life.

5. A gold ring in a pig's snout is a waste of good gold; beauty is wasted on a woman who does not behave wisely.

6. The word "but" connects the two lines of every verse in Proverbs 10.

7. In Proverbs 10:1, the second line describes the opposite of the first.

8. The point of Proverbs 10:1 is that parents are happy with a wise child, saddened by a foolish one.

9. In Proverbs 13:14, the second gives more information about what was said in the first line.

10. The point of Proverbs 13:14 is that teaching from wise people gives life by protecting us from things that would result in death.

11. The second line of Proverbs 4:10 tells the result of obeying the first line's command: the son will live longer.

12. The second line of Proverbs 4:23 gives the reason for obeying the first line's command: everything important in your life comes from your heart.

13. (a); Hiding sin won't pay; confessing sin results in mercy.

14. (a); The one who tries to harm a good man will be harmed, while the good man will have good things.

15. (a); Honesty and poverty are better than cheating and wealth.

16. (s); A person who likes to quarrel provides fuel for disagreements between people.

17. (s); A fool does—again!—what is not only not worth doing, but is harmful to do.

18. (s); A person can harm others very seriously with deceptions he thinks are funny.

19. (a); Faithfully doing the right thing will bring the best rewards, but if riches are your top priority, you'll do what will bring punishment in order to get rich.

20. (a); Hard, faithful work is the way to have what you need; wasting your time on what is worthless leaves you lacking what you need.

21. (S); It's tempting to listen to gossip, but what you hear becomes a part of you and affects how you think and act.

22. (a); A true friend is willing to hurt his friend to help him, but you can't trust the nice things an enemy says or does.

23. (s); Some people respond to correction by trying to harm the corrector.

24. (S); Try to argue with a fool and you'll end up sounding foolish like him.

25. (S); As you make your plans, remember some things are not under your control.

26. Synonymous.

27. Antithetical.

28. Synthetic.

29. Synonymous.

30. Synthetic.

31. Synonymous.

32. Synonymous.

33. A synthetic parallel.

Proverbs

Proverbs 1–31

1. The book's target audience is "the simple," and "the youth."

2. Wisdom.

3. Instruction.

4. Words of insight.

5. Wise dealing.

6. Righteousness

7. Justice

8. Equity.

9. Prudence.

10. Knowledge.

11. Discretion.

12. Increase in learning.

13. Obtain guidance.

14. "The fear of the LORD is the beginning of knowledge; fools despise wisdom and instruction."

15. The father urges his son not to give in to sinful companions who want him to do wrong.

16. Wisdom is compared to a woman calling out in the streets for people to choose her.

17. The Lord gives wisdom.

18. The son should receive the father's words and treasure up his commandments.

19. The son should call out and raise his voice for insight and understanding; he should seek it like silver and search for it as for hidden treasure.

Psalms

Book 1: Psalms 1–41

1. Psalm 1 contrasts the righteous and the wicked.

2. The blessed man delights in the law of the Lord; he meditates on it day and night.

3. Psalm 2 describes the kings of the earth as setting themselves against God to rebel.

4. God responds by laughing at the would-be rebels.

5. God will speak to these rebels in his fury.

6. God will set his King on Zion.

7. "My God, my God, why have you forsaken me?"

8. The mockers said, "Let God deliver him since he delights in him so much!"

9. The enemies divided up this person's clothes, and cast lots for them.

10. People from "all the ends of the earth" would turn to the Lord.

11. Families from the nations would worship before the Lord.

12. In Psalm 32, the blessed person is the one whose transgression is forgiven, whose sin is covered.

13. The Lord's hand was heavy on the psalmist while he kept silent.

14. When the psalmist confessed his transgressions, the Lord forgave his sin.

15. The last verse of Psalm 41: "Blessed be the LORD, the God of Israel, from everlasting to everlasting! Amen and Amen."

Book 2: Psalms 42–72

Book 2: Psalms 42–72

1. The sons of Korah wrote Psalms 42–49.

2. Asaph wrote Psalm 50.

3. The catastrophes in Psalm 42:2 are the earth giving way and the mountains moving into the heart of the sea.

4. Refuge and strength, a very present help in trouble.

5. Water.

6. Dry and weary.

7. Life.

8. Fat and rich food.

9. Solomon wrote Psalm 72.

10. Psalm 72:18: "Blessed be the LORD, the God of Israel, who alone does wondrous things."

Book 3: Psalms 73–89

Book 3: Psalms 73–89

1. Asaph was envious at the prosperity of the wicked.

2. Destroy the wicked.

3. Terrors.

4. The psalmist had God himself for his possession.

5. The first question of Psalm 74 is, "Why do you cast us off forever?"

6. Signs.

7. Prophet.

8. Scoff.

9. Revile.

10. Held back.

11. Indignation.

12. Angry.

13. Psalm 88 is different from all other psalms because it contains no praise at all (unless you count God's title at the beginning, "O God of my salvation").

14. David.

15. Cast off.

16. Rejected.

17. Hide yourself.

18. Steadfast love.

19. Psalm 89:52: "Blessed be the LORD forever! Amen and amen."

Book 4: Psalms 90–106

Book 4: Psalms 90–106

1. Moses was Psalm 90's author.

2. Dwelling place.

3. Beginning.

4. End.

5. The person in the first line of Psalm 91 is one who dwells in the shelter of the Most High.

6. The theme is rejoicing because God is the King over all.

7. Save.

8. Gather.

9. Glory.

10. Psalm 106:48: "Blessed be the LORD, the God of Israel, from everlasting to everlasting! And let all the people say, 'Amen!' Praise the LORD!"

Book 5: Psalms 107–150

Book 5: Psalms 107–150

1. People were hungry and without a place to live.

2. People had sinned and sat in darkness as prisoners.

3. People were in danger of shipwreck.

4. The verse repeated four times is "Let them thank the LORD for his steadfast love, for his wondrous works to the children of man!"

5. The wise should consider the steadfast love of the Lord.

6. Psalm 110 says this seat is at God's right hand.

7. That king will rule over his enemies.

8. This king will be a priest forever.

9. Psalm 139 says God knows: everything we do and when we do it (v. 2a); our thoughts (v. 2b); where we go, where we rest, and everything about us (v. 3); everything we say before we say it (v. 4); us, inside and out (v. 1).

10. Psalm 139 says God would be with his people in heaven, in Sheol, as far east as they could go, in the middle of the sea, in darkness, or in light.

11. All the days each of God's people will have are written in God's book.

12. God's thoughts toward each of his people are more than the number of grains of sand.

13. The psalmist wants God to search him and know his heart.

14. Grievous way.

15. Psalms 120-134 all have the heading "A Song of Ascent."

16. The first sentence of the last five psalms is "Praise the LORD!"

17. The last sentence of the last five psalms is "Praise the LORD!"

Ecclesiastes

Ecclesiastes 1–12

1. The Preacher calls himself "son of David, king in Jerusalem."

2. "Vanity of vanities, says the Preacher, vanity of vanities! All is vanity."

3. Striving after wind.

4. "Under the sun."

5. The poem begins with "What does man gain by all the toil at which he toils under the sun?"

6. Full of weariness.

7. "Everything that is done under the sun" is striving after wind.

8. Crooked.

9. Lacking.

10. Sorrow.

11. Striving after wind.

12. Pleasure.

13. In pleasure and toil, nothing is to be gained under the sun.

14. Being wise.

15. Dies.

16. Solomon says hard work is vanity, because all a person works for must be left to someone who did not toil for it.

17. The author complains that there is wickedness even in the place of justice and in the place of righteousness.

18. The author says it is vanity that man dies just like the beasts do.

19. Oppression.

20. Dead.

21. Living.

22. Born.

23. Righteous.

24. Wicked.

25. Wicked.

26. Righteous.

27. "Vanity of vanities, all is vanity."

28. God gave the children of men the "un-happy business" with which they are busy.

29. Fear God.

30. The wicked.

31. Prolong.

32. Enjoyment.

33. Hand of God.

34. Ecclesiastes 3:1: "For everything there is a season, and a time for every matter under heaven."

35. Find out.

36. Joyful.

37. Good.

38. Gift.

39. Rejoice.

40. Judgment.

41. Evil.

42. Creator.

43. Fear.

44. Commandments.

45. Duty.

46. Judgment.

47. Secret.

Song of Solomon

Song of Solomon 1–8

Song of Solomon 1–8

1. Solomon's.

Job

Job 1–42

Job 1–42

1. Job is described as being blameless and upright, fearing God, and turning away from evil.

2. 7,000 sheep.

3. 3,000 camels.

4. 500 yoke of oxen.

5. 500 donkeys.

6. 10 children.

7. God began the conversation between God and Satan.

8. God brought up Job.

9. According to Satan, Job served God because of how God had blessed him.

10. Satan said Job would curse God if he took away his possessions.

11. Satan had to have God's permission before he could do anything against Job.

12. Sabean raiders stole Job's oxen and donkeys, killing the servants who kept them.

13. Fire from heaven fell and burned the sheep and the shepherds.

14. Chaldean raiders stole the camels, after killing the servants.

15. All Job's children died when a wind blew down the house they were in.

16. Job did not sin, or accuse God of wrong.

17. In chapter 2, God initiated the conversation with Satan.

18. God brought up Job.

19. Satan said Job was still faithful to God because his own physical body had not been harmed.

20. Job was covered with loathsome sores from the top of his head to the bottom of his feet.

21. Good.

22. Evil.

23. God had brought upon him.

24. The purpose of Job's three friends was to show Job sympathy and to comfort him.

25. Job cursed the day of his birth.

26. Job wondered why he had been born.

27. Eliphaz was the first of Job's friends to speak to him.

28. Iniquity.

29. Trouble.

30. Bildad spoke to Job next.

31. Sinned against him.

32. Sudden death.

33. The wicked.

34. God is the "he" in this passage.

35. "If it is not he [God], who then is it?"

36. Job said God favors the designs of the wicked.

37. Zophar spoke next.

38. "Though he slay me, I will hope in him."

39. Job's incorrect assumption was that God counted Job as his enemy.

40. We know this isn't true from God's comments to Satan about how pleased he was with Job.

41. Job said God hated him and called God "my adversary."

42. Answer.

43. Cruel.

44. Persecuted.

45. Lied.

46. Mistreated his servants.

47. Refused to help the poor.

48. Trusted in his wealth or been proud of it.

49. Rejoiced in an enemy's misfortune.

50. Covered up sins.

51. The earth.

52. Sea.

53. No farther.

54. The morning.

55. The snow.

56. Lightnings.

57. Lion.

58. Raven.

59. Hawk.

60. Mounts up.

61. No further.

62. Job said he was of small account.

63. Did not understand.

64. Wonderful for me.

65. I did not know.

66. Repent.

67. God told Job's three friends that his anger burned against them for speaking what was not right about him.

68. When Job prayed for his friends, God restored Job's fortunes.

69. 14,000 sheep.

70. 6,000 camels.

71. 1,000 yoke of oxen.

72. 1,000 donkeys.

Test 13
The Poetry Books

Short answer.

1. Parallelism.

2. Five.

3. Songs; hymnbook.

4. The opposite of what was described in the first line.

5. The simple or youth.

6. He wanted them to gain wisdom, knowledge, and understanding.

7. Solomon.

8. The fear of the Lord.

9. David.

10. Solomon.

11. Love.

12. Married love.

13. Says the same thing as the first line, in a different way.

14. Vanity.

15. Life here and now, in a fallen world affected by sin.

16. We should trust God and enjoy what he has given, fearing and obeying him in light of judgment to come.

17. Wisdom.

18. A promise guarantees that what it said will happen; a proverb is an observation of what usually happens in certain situations.

19. Adds to what was said in the first line.

20. Satan accused Job of serving God for what he got out of it.

21. Job's three friends said Job's suffering was the result of great sin on his part.

22. He burned with anger that they had spoken what was not right about him.

23. How God was dealing with him.

24. God showed Job many things God can do that Job could not to make it clear that God has much greater wisdom and power than Job did, so Job needed to trust him.

25. Double of all that Job had had before.

Volume 3: The New Testament

The Gospel According to Luke

Luke 1–2

Luke 1–2

1. An orderly account.

2. Certainty concerning the things he'd been taught.

3. Those who, from the beginning, were eyewitnesses and ministers of the Word.

4. Zechariah was in the temple, offering incense.

5. Zechariah was troubled and filled with fear.

6. Zechariah was struck dumb.

7. Mary.

8. Mary was troubled.

9. Jesus.

10. The baby will have the throne of his father David; he will rule over the house of Jacob.

11. God.

12. The fathers.

13. Abraham.

14. In the house of David.

15. The prophets.

16. Our fathers.

17. His holy covenant.

18. Abraham.

19. Serve God.

20. Fear.

21. Holiness and righteousness.

22. The Lord.

23. Prepare his way.

24. Forgiveness.

25. Tender mercy.

26. Darkness.

27. The shadow of death.

28. The way of peace.

29. A great joy.

30. All the people.

31. Savior.

32. Christ the Lord.

33. The consolation of Israel.

34. Simeon wouldn't die until he had seen the Lord's Christ (or "anointed" or "Messiah").

35. God's salvation.

36. The Gentiles.

37. God's people Israel.

38. Simeon said the child was appointed for the fall and rising of many in Israel, and for a sign that is opposed.

Luke 3–7

1. The purpose of John's baptism was to show repentance for the forgiveness of sins.

2. People were wondering about John: "Could he be the Christ?"

3. The one coming after John would baptize with the Holy Spirit and with fire.

4. Herod had John the Baptist imprisoned because John had reproved Herod for all the evil he had done.

5. The Holy Spirit, in the form of a dove.

6. God's voice was heard, saying, "You are my beloved Son."

7. Jesus was in the wilderness forty days; he was tempted by Satan while he was there.

8. The Holy Spirit.

9. Jesus used Scripture.

10. Deuteronomy.

11. Isaiah 61:1-2.

12. Jesus said of the passage, "Today this Scripture has been fulfilled in your hearing."

13. The angry crowd intended to throw Jesus off a cliff.

14. Jesus passed through the middle of the angry crowd and went away.

15. Capernaum.

16. What astonished people about Jesus' teaching was the authority it had.

17. Jesus rebuked the unclean demon.

18. The people said, "With authority and power he commands the unclean spirits, and they come out."

19. The Sabbath.

20. Jesus also rebuked the fever of Peter's mother-in-law and more demons.

21. Jesus did his teaching from a boat just offshore.

22. Peter responded to the great catch of fish by falling down at Jesus' knees, crying, "Depart from me, for I am a sinful man, O Lord."

23. Peter, Andrew, James, and John.

24. They left everything to follow him.

25. Yes.

26. He wasn't sure that Jesus wanted to.

27. Jesus healed the leper by touching him.

28. Mark wrote that Jesus was moved with pity for the leper.

29. Will.

30. Clean.

31. Hear him and to be healed of their infirmities.

32. Jesus withdrew to lonely places to pray.

33. The man whose friends brought him to Jesus was paralyzed.

34. "Your sins are forgiven you."

35. The Pharisees thought Jesus was speaking blasphemies.

36. Jesus healed the paralyzed man to show that he had authority to forgive sins.

37. The people were filled with awe and glorified God.

38. At his tax booth.

39. Levi left everything and followed Jesus.

40. Tax collectors and others were at Levi's feast for Jesus.

41. The Pharisees complained that Jesus shouldn't eat with bad people like these.

42. Jesus.

43. The Pharisees complained that Jesus—and his disciples—were breaking the Sabbath.

44. Lord of the Sabbath.

45. To do good, to save life.

46. The Pharisees were filled with fury.

47. Before choosing his disciples, Jesus spent the whole night in prayer.

48. Luke 6:31.

49. Love.

50. Tunics.

51. Nothing in return.

52. Your reward will be great; you will be Sons of the Most High.

53. A man trying to remove a speck from someone's eye while a whole log is sticking out of his own eye.

54. As a rotten tree can only produce rotten fruit, so a bad heart can only produce bad actions.

55. The foolish man represents the one who hears Jesus' teaching but doesn't act upon it.

56. The wise man represents the one who hears Jesus' teaching and does what he says.

57. The Jewish elders thought the centurion was worthy of Jesus' help.

58. The centurion thought he was not worthy of Jesus' being in his home.

59. The centurion believed Jesus could heal his servant with just a word.

60. A funeral procession.

61. Death.

62. Jesus told John's disciples to tell John of the many miracles Jesus did.

63. The Pharisee who had invited Jesus to dinner criticized Jesus for letting the woman wash his feet.

64. Forgiven.

65. Loved.

66. Loved.

67. Forgiven.

68. Jesus said, "Your sins are forgiven."

69. The people responded with, "Who is this, who even forgives sins?"

Luke
8–12

Luke 8–12

1. Mary Magdalene, Joanna the wife of Chuza, Herod's household manager, Susanna, many others.

2. The Word of God.

3. Hear.

4. The devil.

5. Receive.

6. Joy.

7. Root.

8. Testing.

9. Choked out.

10. Cares.

11. Riches.

12. Pleasures of this life.

13. Mature.

14. Hear.

15. Hold it fast.

16. Bear fruit.

17. Patience.

18. Jesus called those who hear the Word of God and do it his mother and brothers.

19. He fell asleep.

20. He commanded the wind and the raging waves.

21. Rebuked.

22. "Who is this, that he commands even winds and water, and they obey him?"

23. Afraid.

24. The man who met Jesus was naked; he lived in the tombs; he was kept in chains, which he would break.

25. The man's name was Legion because so many demons lived in him.

26. The demons entered a herd of pigs.

27. People saw the man clothed, in his right mind, and sitting at Jesus' feet.

28. Jesus told the man to declare "how much God has done for you."

29. The man proclaimed how much Jesus had done for him.

30. Jesus raised a dead girl back to life.

31. Jesus showed himself to be Lord over wind and waves.

32. Herod wondered, "Who is this about whom I hear such things?"

33. "Who do the crowds say that I am?"

34. "Elijah or John the Baptist or one of the prophets of old."

35. "The Christ of God."

36. Jesus said he must suffer, be rejected, be killed, be raised.

37. The disciples didn't understand.

38. Jesus set his face to go to Jerusalem.

39. On the mountain, Jesus' face was altered and his clothing became dazzling white.

40. Glory.

41. The two men were Moses and Elijah.

42. Jesus, Moses, and Elijah were discussing Jesus' departure, which he was about to accomplish at Jerusalem.

43. His glory.

44. Majesty.

45. To follow Christ, one must deny himself.

46. He must take up his cross.

47. Daily.

48. "Whoever would save his life will lose it, but whoever loses his life for my sake will save it."

49. Jesus told his first would-be follower that he might not have even a place to stay.

50. The disciples were rejoicing because the demons were subject to them in Jesus' name.

51. Because their names were written in heaven.

52. The wise and understanding.

53. To little children.

54. Gracious will.

55. To put Jesus to the test.

56. To justify himself.

57. "Which of these proved to be a neighbor to the man who fell among robbers?"

58. Jesus' disciples asked him to teach them how to pray.

59. Hallowed.

60. Kingdom.

61. Our daily bread.

62. Sins.

63. Temptation.

64. Jesus taught that God answers prayer, and that we should persevere in asking for what we need.

65. With me

66. Against.

67. Gather.

68. Scatters.

69. Sodom.

70. Receive.

71. Tyre.

72. Sidon.

73. Repented.

74. Mighty works.

75. Queen of the South.

76. The ends of the earth.

77. Greater.

78. Nineveh.

79. Repented.

80. Greater.

81. Hear the Word of God

82. Keep.

83. Jesus said the harsh things about the Pharisees at dinner in the home of a Pharisee.

84. There were thousands of people around Jesus.

85. To his disciples.

86. Someone in the crowd wanted Jesus to tell his brother to share the inheritance with him.

87. Covetousness.

88. The abundance of possessions.

89. This man failed to be rich toward God.

90. A fool.

91. Food and clothing.

92. The birds.

93. The flowers.

94. All the nations of the earth have to seek for these things.

95. God's kingdom.

96. His coming.

97. Peace on earth.

98. Division.

Luke 13–18

1. The woman was bent over and could not stand up straight.

2. Jesus healed her in the synagogue on the Sabbath.

3. Hypocrites.

4. Jesus' adversaries were put to shame.

5. The people rejoiced at what Jesus was doing.

6. Jesus healed the man in a Pharisee ruler's house on the Sabbath.

7. Jesus healed ten men of leprosy.

8. The man who returned to thank Jesus was a Samaritan.

9. The blind man Jesus healed was by the side of the road, on the way into Jericho.

10. He cried out all the more.

11. The point of the parable in 13:6-9 was that God graciously waits for people to repent but judgment will come at last; people should take advantage of God's patience and repent now while they can.

12. God.

13. Sinful people.

14. Repentance and obedience.

15. The kingdom of God is like a mustard seed because it starts very small and becomes very big.

16. The kingdom of God is like yeast in flour because it is small and hard to see, but it mixes in with the rest and affects it all.

17. The main point of the parable in 14:7–11: Don't seek honor for yourself; take the lowly place.

18. Jerusalem.

19. "Will those who are saved be few?"

20. The narrow gate.

21. Not be able to.

22. Depart from me.

23. "Blessed is everyone who will eat bread in the kingdom of God."

24. The invited banquet guests made excuses about why they could not come.

25. When invited, the poor and crippled and blind and lame came, and even those out in the highways and hedges.

26. Tax collectors and sinners.

27. By grumbling and saying, "This man receives sinners."

28. A shepherd rejoiced when he found his lost sheep.

29. A woman rejoiced when she found her lost coin.

30. One repentant sinner.

31. The older brother.

32. The one who has been faithful in little things.

33. God and money.

34. The Pharisees ridiculed Jesus because they loved money.

35. Abraham's answer was that the rich man's brothers had all they needed in Moses and the prophets—God's Word; they should hear them.

36. We ought always to pray and not lose heart.

37. The Pharisee expected that he would earn God's favor by all his righteous/religious acts.

38. God's mercy.

39. Justified.

40. Because great crowds were following him.

41. Parents, children, spouse, siblings, even one's own life.

42. All he has.

43. Salt with no saltiness.

44. The servant had to clean up, dress up, cook the dinner, and go serve the boss.

45. "We are unworthy servants; we have only done what was our duty."

46. The Pharisees asked Jesus when the kingdom of God would come.

47. In the midst of you.

48. Children.

49. They rebuked the people who had brought the children.

50. Jesus was indignant with his disciples.

51. In his arms.

52. Laying his hands.

53. The rich young ruler's response was, "I've kept them all from my youth."

54. Jesus told the rich young ruler that he still had to sell everything and give to the poor.

55. Jesus said his disciples, who had left everything for him, would receive many times more, in this life and in the age to come.

56. Jesus said he must suffer and be rejected.

57. Jesus said that, in Jerusalem, everything written about the Son of Man would be accomplished.

58. Specifically, Jesus said he would be mocked and shamefully treated and spit upon, flogged, and killed; but on the third day, he would rise.

Luke 19–24

Luke 19–24

1. "I must stay at your house today."

2. Zacchaeus received Jesus joyfully.

3. Jesus said salvation had come to Zacchaeus's house.

4. As evidence of Zacchaeus's conversion, he said he would pay back four times those he had cheated, and he would give half of what he had to the poor.

5. A mina.

6. One servant was condemned because he did nothing for the master with his mina.

7. Jesus.

8. Those unbelievers who refuse Jesus' rule.

9. He wept.

10. He drove out those who were selling things.

11. Jesus taught.

12. The chief priests and scribes responded by looking for a way to destroy Jesus.

13. God.

14. The scribes and Pharisees, the leaders of the Jews.

15. The prophets.

16. Jesus.

17. The landowner would destroy those renters and give the vineyard to others.

18. The scribes and chief priests realized that Jesus had told the parable about them.

19. The Jewish leaders were the builders; Jesus was the cornerstone.

20. Any who fell on the stone would be broken to pieces.

21. Any on whom the stone fell would be crushed.

22. Because the others had given what they didn't need for themselves; the widow gave all she had to live on.

23. Son of Man.

24. Watch.

25. Dissipation.

26. Drunkenness.

27. Cares of this life.

28. Trap.

29. "This is my body, which is given for you. Do this in remembrance of me."

30. "This cup that is poured out for you is the new covenant in my blood."

31. Been determined.

32. Woe.

33. The cup to be removed from him.

34. Not my will, but yours be done."

35. Cut off a servant's ear with his sword, and Jesus healed the ear.

36. Simon of Cyrene.

37. To remember him when he came into his kingdom.

38. The thief said he was receiving the due reward of his deed.

39. "Today you will be with me in Paradise."

40. The curtain of the temple was torn in two.

41. "Father, into your hands I commit my spirit."

42. The centurion.

43. "He breathed his last."

44. "Yielded up his spirit."

45. "Gave up his spirit."

46. Joseph of Arimathea asked for Jesus' body; he was a member of the council.

47. Mary Magdalene, Joanna, Mary the mother of James, and other women were the first to hear that Jesus had risen; they heard it from two angels.

48. The disciples didn't believe the women at first.

49. Peter.

50. Peter saw the linen cloths lying by themselves.

51. They had hoped the man who had been crucified was the one to redeem Israel.

52. Himself.

53. These things about Jesus were in all the Scriptures.

54. Jesus began with Moses and the prophets.

55. Jesus had opened to them the Scriptures.

56. In the Law of Moses and the Prophets and the Psalms.

57. Fulfilled.

58. Jesus opened the disciples' minds to understand the Scriptures.

59. His hands and feet.

60. To touch him.

61. Something to eat.

62. Repentance and forgiveness of sin.

63. In Jerusalem.

64. Power from on high.

65. Promise of the Father.

Fulfilled Prophecies in Matthew's Gospel

Matthew 1–24

Matthew 1–24

1. "A virgin shall conceive and bear a son and they shall call his name Immanuel."

2. Ruler.

3. Bethlehem.

4. Shepherd.

5. "Out of Egypt I called my son."

6. Matthew said Jeremiah's prophecy of Jewish women weeping for their children was fulfilled when Herod slaughtered all the boy babies in Bethlehem.

7. John the Baptist.

8. Isaiah.

9. The voice of one crying in the wilderness: "Prepare the way of the Lord; make his paths straight."

10. Zebulun.

11. Naphtali.

12. Galilee.

13. Jesus withdrew into Galilee, and went and lived in Capernaum, in the territory of Zebulun and Naphtali.

14. What was spoken by the prophet Isaiah might be fulfilled.

15. Oppressed by demons.

16. With a word.

17. Healed.

18. Sick.

19. Isaiah.

20. Illnesses.

21. Diseases.

22. Jesus ordered those whom he healed not to make him known.

23. Aloud.

24. Hear his voice.

25. Understand.

26. Perceive.

27. Isaiah's.

28. Dull.

29. Hear.

30. Closed.

31. See.

32. Hear.

33. Heart.

34. Turn.

35. Heal.

36. In parables.

37. Nothing.

38. Matthew said Jesus spoke in parables to fulfill what was spoken by the prophet.

39. Parables.

40. Hidden.

41. With their mouths.

42. With their lips.

43. Their hearts.

44. A commandment taught by men.

45. "Why do your disciples break the traditions of the elders?"

46. Jesus said the Pharisees broke God's commandment for the sake of their tradition.

47. The Pharisees and scribes.

48. The chariot.

49. The war horse.

50. The battle bow.

51. Peace.

52. His rule would be from sea to sea, to the ends of the earth.

53. A donkey.

54. To fulfill what was spoken by the prophet.

55. The mouths of babies and infants.

56. "Hosanna to the Son of David!"

57. "Out of the mouths of infants and nursing babies you have prepared praise."

58. Rejected.

59. Cornerstone.

60. The Lord's.

61. Marvelous.

62. His shepherd.

63. The sheep.

64. Just before Jesus was arrested, he told his disciples they would all fall away.

65. Jesus said this would happen because it was written, "I will strike the shepherd and the sheep of the flock will be scattered."

66. Because then the Scriptures couldn't have been fulfilled.

67. "But all this has taken place that the Scriptures of the prophets might be fulfilled."

68. Jeremiah.

69. Thirty pieces of silver.

1. Believe.
2. The Christ.
3. Son of God.
4. Believing.
5. Life.
6. Name.

John 1–3

John 1–3

1. John 1:14.
2. The beginning.
3. With.
4. Was.
5. Made.
6. Life.
7. The light.
8. Children.
9. Flesh.
10. Glory.
11. Grace.
12. Truth.
13. Seen.
14. The lamb of God.
15. Takes away the sin of the world.
16. Andrew.
17. Simon Peter.
18. Nathanael.
19. The Son of Man.
20. Jesus turned water into wine at a wedding.
21. The first of his signs.
22. Jesus' glory.
23. Jesus' disciples believed in him.
24. John told the story of Jesus driving sellers and money changers from the temple.
25. A person must be born again to see the kingdom of God.
26. Jesus alluded to the story of the serpent in the wilderness, lifted up by Moses.
27. Jesus said the person who does not believe is condemned already.

John 4–7

John 4–7

1. Had.
2. Jesus used a request for a drink to get a conversation going with the Samaritan woman.
3. Water that would keep her from ever being thirsty again.
4. "I who speak to you am he."

5. No.

6. "Go, your son will live."

7. The second sign Jesus did.

8. An invalid.

9. 38 years.

10. The Sabbath.

11. The Jews were seeking to kill Jesus.

12. Calling God his own Father.

13. Equal with God.

14. Fed 5,000+ people with five loaves and two fish.

15. Walked on water.

16. The Bread of Life.

17. Hunger.

18. Thirst.

19. His flesh.

20. Live.

21. Live.

22. Feeds on him.

23. Eats.

24. Drinks.

25. The Father.

26. From heaven.

27. Many of Jesus' "disciples" turned back and no longer followed him.

28. Can.

29. Draws.

30. Thirsts, let him come to me and drink.

31. Out of his heart will flow rivers of living water.

32. The Holy Spirit.

33. Glorified.

John 8–10

John 8–10

1. The light of the world.

2. Jesus said, "I always do the things that are pleasing to him."

3. Jesus asked his enemies, "Which of you convicts me of sin?"

4. Jesus answered, "Truly, truly, I say to you, before Abraham was, I am."

5. The Jews picked up stones to stone him.

6. Man born blind.

7. The door of the sheep.

8. The Good Shepherd.

9. Lays down his life.

10. Hear his voice.

11. Follow him.

12. Jesus would give his sheep eternal life.

13. No one would ever be able to snatch his sheep out of Jesus' hand.

14. They were not of his flock.

15. Jesus said, "I and the Father are one," and again the Jews took up stones to stone him.

John 11–12

John 11–12

1. Jesus was beyond the Jordan where John had been baptizing.

2. In Bethany.

3. Jesus loved this family.

4. Jesus stayed two days longer in the place where he was.

5. "Let's go to Judea again."

6. He was going to wake Lazarus.

7. Lazarus had been dead four days.

8. "Lord, if you had been here, my brother would not have died."

9. The resurrection.

10. The life.

11. Shall he live.

12. Jesus said the person who lived and believed in him would never die.

13. "Lord, if you had been here, my brother would not have died."

14. Jesus was deeply moved in his spirit and greatly troubled.

15. Jesus wept.

16. Jesus cried out, "Lazarus, come out."

17. Raised Lazarus from the dead.

18. Many of the Jews believed in Jesus, but some went to the Pharisees to tell them about it.

19. One man should die for the people, not that the whole nation should perish.

20. 300 denarii.

21. The moneybag.

22. He used to help himself to what was put into it.

23. Comes in the name of the Lord.

24. King of Israel.

25. The Greeks told Philip they wanted to see Jesus.

26. The Son of Man to be glorified.

27. It will bear much fruit.

28. Jesus said a disciple would have to hate his life in this world if he wanted to keep it for eternity.

29. Jesus said his heart was troubled.

30. Jesus wouldn't ask his Father to save him from that hour because he had come on purpose for that hour.

31. Instead, Jesus asked the Father to glorify his name.

32. Jesus said the ruler of this world would be cast out.

33. He would draw all people to himself.

34. So many signs.

35. Did not believe in him.

John 13–17

John 13–17

1. Jesus knew that his hour had come to depart out of this world to his Father.

2. Jesus had loved his disciples, and he would love them to the end.

3. Jesus also knew that the Father had given all things into his hands, and that he had come from God and was going back to God.

4. Jesus washed his disciples' feet.

5. Lord and Teacher.

6. Also ought to wash one another's feet.

7. An example.

8. As I have done to you.

9. Know.

10. You do them.

11. Love one another.

12. Have loved you.

13. Love one another.

14. Love for each other.

15. Jesus was going so he could prepare a place for his followers in his Father's house.

16. Later, Jesus would come again and take his followers to himself.

17. The way.

18. The truth.

19. The life.

20. No one.

21. Through me.

22. The disciples would do greater works than those he had done.

23. The Holy Spirit.

24. Forever.

25. With God's people, and he would be in them.

26. The Holy Spirit would teach the apostles all things and bring to their remembrance all that Jesus had said.

27. The one who loves Jesus is the one who has his commandments and keeps them.

28. The true Vine.

29. God's Old Testament people, Israel, are the vine he planted, which failed to produce good fruit.

30. Branches.

31. Produces much fruit.

32. Ten.

33. We prove we are Christ's disciples when we bear much fruit.

34. None.

35. The branch that doesn't bear fruit is thrown away, then burned.

36. The branch that does bear fruit is pruned.

37. The vinedresser, God the Father, prunes the branch so it will bear more fruit.

38. Love each other.

39. Has loved them.

40. Jesus showed his love for his people by laying down his life for them.

41. Choose me.

42. Chose you.

43. Bear fruit.

44. Persecute them.

45. The Holy Spirit would bear witness about Jesus.

46. Advantage.

47. Send.

48. Jesus said his disciples would have sorrow, but their sorrow would be turned to joy.

49. The purpose was giving eternal life to all whom God had given him.

50. Jesus defined eternal life as knowing the only true God and Jesus Christ, whom he had sent.

51. So that he (Jesus) might glorify the Father.

52. The world.	61. The truth.
53. The Father had given him.	62. God's Word.
54. Received.	63. Believe in him.
55. God had sent him.	64. The Word.
56. Keep them.	65. One.
57. Be one.	66. Believe.
58. Take them out of the world.	67. With him.
59. The evil one.	68. See his glory.
60. Sanctify.	69. Before the foundation of the world.

John 18–21

1. I am he.

2. The disciple whom he loved.

3. The soldier pierced Jesus' side with a spear.

4. Mary Magdalene first found the tomb empty, followed by Peter and John.

5. Mary Magdalene saw Jesus near the tomb.

6. The disciples had the doors locked for fear of the Jews.

7. Thomas.

8. See.

9. Mark of the nails.

10. Place his finger.

11. Mark of the nails.

12. His side.

13. "My Lord and my God!"

14. The person on the shore told the disciples where to put their nets, and they caught so many fish that they couldn't haul the net back in.

15. "Do you love me?"

16. Three times; "Feed my sheep."

17. Jesus had done so many other things that all the books in the world could not contain them all.

Test 1

The Gospels

Matching.

1. J. L.

2. M.

3. H.

4. B. E. G.

5. I.

6. A. D.

7. C.

8. F. N.

9. K.

From Matthew's Gospel.

Short answer.

10. A virgin conceived and had a son; God's king was born in Bethlehem; God's son went to Egypt for a time; women in Bethlehem wept for their children when Herod killed them.

11. John the Baptist was the "voice of one crying in the wilderness" to prepare for the Messiah; light shone on Galilee when Jesus lived and ministered there; God's servant bore our sicknesses when Jesus healed many; Jesus told people he healed to keep it secret (God's servant wouldn't cry out or lift his voice); Jesus spoke in parables so people would hear without understanding; the Pharisees of Jesus' day honored men's traditions more than God's commands.

12. Jesus rode into Jerusalem on a donkey; praise came from the mouths of children; Jesus (the cornerstone) was rejected by the builders (the Jewish leaders); the shepherd (Jesus) was taken and the sheep (the disciples) were scattered; Jesus was arrested, condemned, and put to death; Jesus was sold for thirty pieces of silver.

From John's Gospel.

13. Seven signs: changing of water into wine; healing of the official's son from a distance; healing of a man who had been an invalid for 38 years; feeding of 5,000; walking on the sea; healing of the man born blind; raising of Lazarus from the dead.

14. Seven "I am's": I am the bread of life; I am the Light of the World; I am the door of the sheep; I am the Good Shepherd; I am the resurrection and the life; I am the Way, the Truth, and the Life; I am the true Vine.

Fill in the blanks.

15. Person, natures.

16. Jesus' upcoming departure (death) in Jerusalem.

17. "Who is this?" or "Who is Jesus?"

18. Gospel; "good news."

19. Same view; Matthew, Mark, Luke.

20. Peace throughout the empire; an excellent system of roads.

21. The Greek language.

22. "God saves"; Messiah, "God's anointed."

23. Christ-centered.

Gospels.

24. Jn.	**29.** Mk.	**34.** Mk.	**39.** Jn.
25. Mt.	**30.** Mt.	**35.** Jn.	**40.** Jn.
26. Lk.	**31.** Lk.	**36.** Mk.	
27. Lk.	**32.** Mt.	**37** Lk.	
28. Jn.	**33.** Lk.	**38.** Lk.	

Acts 1:1–6:7

Acts 1:1–6:7

1. Theophilus.

2. Jesus began to do and teach.

3. The day when he was taken up.

4. Power.

5. Holy Spirit.

6. Not many days from now.

7. They were to be his witnesses in Jerusalem, all Judea and Samaria, and to the end of the earth.

8. Proclaiming.

9. The Lord Jesus Christ.

10. Boldness.

11. Hindrance.

12. They were filled with the Holy Spirit.

13. Tongues as of fire appeared and rested on each person.

14. A sound like a mighty rushing wind was heard, and people spoke in languages (tongues) they had never learned.

15. Every nation under heaven.

16. These visitors were hearing Jesus' followers telling the mighty works of God in their own languages.

17. Peter.

18. Joel.

19. And in the last days.

20. God was pouring out his Spirit on all kinds of people, as he had promised.

21. Call upon the name of the Lord.

22. Saved.

23. The definite plan and foreknowledge of God.

24. Lawless men.

25. Lord.

26. Christ.

27. You crucified.

28. Peter's hearers were cut to the heart and cried out, "What shall we do?"

29. Peter told them to repent and be baptized in the name of Jesus for the forgiveness of their sins.

30. 3,000 people.

31. The believers in Jerusalem devoted themselves to the apostles' teaching and the fellowship, to the breaking of bread (the Lord's Supper) and the prayers.

32. The Lord added to their number day by day those who were being saved.

33. Money.

34. Peter healed him instead.

35. The Holy and Righteous One.

36. The Author of life.

37. Repent.

38. Prophet.

39. Moses.

40. Destroyed from the people.

41. Covenant.

42. Abraham.

43. Of the earth.

44. Offspring.

45. Turning.

46. Their wickedness.

47. Priests and other leaders were greatly annoyed, but many who heard Peter believed.

48. Peter and John were arrested and put in jail overnight.

49. 5,000.

50. Peter was filled with the Holy Spirit.

51. Peter described Jesus as crucified by the people to whom he was speaking, but raised from the dead by God.

52. Peter called Jesus the stone rejected by the builders and the cornerstone; he called the Jewish leaders the builders who had rejected him.

53. Acts 4:12: "There is salvation in no one else, for there is no other name under heaven given among men by which we must be saved."

54. Speak or teach at all in the name of Jesus.

55. Peter and John answered that they must listen to God, rather than to these Jewish leaders.

56. They prayed.

57. To the "sovereign Lord."

58. Hand.

59. Plan.

60. Predestined.

61. The ability to continue to speak God's Word with boldness.

62. Filled with the Holy Spirit.

63. Speak the Word of God with boldness.

64. They shared their possessions with each other; they had everything in common.

65. Son of encouragement.

66. Barnabas gave the apostles the money he had made from selling his field.

67. Ananias and Sapphira gave some of their money to the apostles; the rest they kept back for themselves.

68. The Holy Spirit.

69. To God.

70. Ananias fell dead immediately.

71. Sapphira fell down dead.

72. Great fear fell upon them.

73. People in Jerusalem didn't dare to join the Christians, but they held the believers in high esteem.

74. Multitudes.

75. The high priest and the Sadducees were filled with jealousy; they arrested the apostles and put them in jail.

76. In the night, an angel of the Lord opened the prison and brought the apostles out.

77. Speak to the people, in the temple, all the words of this Life (the gospel).

78. "We must obey God rather than man."

79. Exalted.

80. Leader.

81. Savior.

82. Repentance.

83. Forgiveness of sins.

84. The Holy Spirit.

85. The leaders wanted to kill the apostles.

86. The leaders beat the apostles and charged them not to speak in Jesus' name.

87. The apostles rejoiced because they were counted worthy to suffer dishonor for Jesus' name.

88. The apostles did not cease teaching and preaching Jesus as the Christ.

89. The complaint was by the Hellenists, against the Hebrews, because the Hellenistic widows were being neglected in the daily distribution (of food).

90. To make sure food was handed out correctly, the apostles told the church to choose seven men to oversee it.

91. The apostles intended to devote themselves to prayer and to the ministry of the Word.

92. Increase.

93. Multiplied greatly.

94. Jerusalem.

95. Priests.

96. Obedient to the faith.

Acts 6:8–9:31

Acts 6:8–9:31

1. Stephen.

2. Because of the wisdom and the Spirit with which he spoke.

3. Stephen was full of the Holy Spirit.

4. Stephen said he saw the Son of Man standing at the right hand of God.

5. Stephen's enemies stoned him to death, and Saul watched their cloaks while they did.

6. Saul approved of Stephen's execution.

7. A great persecution arose against the church in Jerusalem.

8. Saul was entering house after house, dragging off men and women to prison.

9. All the Christians except the apostles left Jerusalem and were scattered throughout the regions of Judea and Samaria.

10. They went about preaching the Word.

11. Philip went to the city of Samaria; he proclaimed to them the Christ.

12. Many Samaritans were believing and being baptized.

13. Peter and John came to pray for the Samaritan believers because the Holy Spirit had not fallen on them.

14. Simon offered them money in exchange for the ability to give the Holy Spirit to people.

15. Philip met a man from Ethiopia who worked for Candace, queen of the Ethiopians.

16. He was reading from the prophet Isaiah.

17. Philip told the man the good news about Jesus.

18. To be baptized.

19. Philip preached the gospel in all the towns he passed through.

20. To find more Christians to bring bound to Jerusalem.

21. A light from heaven flashing around him.

22. The voice of Jesus.

23. In the city, Saul would be told what he was to do.

24. Ananias did not want to go to Saul.

25. Chosen instrument.

26. Gentiles.

27. The Lord would show Saul how much he would have to suffer for the sake of Jesus' name.

28. Ananias said the Lord had sent him so that Saul could regain his sight and be filled with the Holy Spirit.

29. Immediately, Saul proclaimed Jesus in the synagogues, saying, "He is the Son of God."

30. Judea.

31. Galilee.

32. Samaria.

33. Built up.

34. Fear of the Lord.

35. Comfort of the Holy Spirit.

36. Multiplied.

Acts 9:32–12:24

**Acts
9:32–12:24**

1. All kinds of animals, birds, and reptiles.

2. "What God has made clean, do not call common."

3. The men took Peter to the house of Cornelius, a Roman centurion.

4. Peter understood that God shows no partiality.

5. The Holy Spirit fell on those who heard.

6. Gave the same gift.

7. Should stand in God's way.

8. Repentance that leads to life.

9. As far as Phoenicia and Cyprus and Antioch.

10. Jews.

11. A great number.

12. He went to Tarsus and picked up Saul.

13. Christians.

14. James.

15. Herod arrested Peter, planning to "bring him out to the people" (kill him too) after the Passover.

16. The church made earnest prayer to God for Peter.

17. Peter was chained with two chains, with a soldier on either side of him, and there were guards at the doors.

18. An angel of the Lord awakened Peter.

19. Peter's chains fell off.

20. No.

21. They opened of their own accord.

22. Mary, the mother of John Mark.

23. "You are out of your mind!"

24. Herod's listeners responded to him by shouting, "The voice of a god and not a man!"

25. Herod failed to give glory to God, and immediately an angel struck him and he was eaten by worms and died.

26. "The word of God increased and multiplied."

The Epistle of James

James 1–5

James
1–5

1. A servant of God and of the Lord Jesus Christ.

2. Testing.

3. Steadfastness.

4. Perfect.

5. Complete.

6. The believer who lacks wisdom should ask of God, without doubting.

7. The crown of life.

8. Temptations to sin don't come from God because God cannot be tempted with evil, and he doesn't tempt anyone.

9. People are tempted by their own desire.

10. Every good and perfect gift comes from God.

11. God's character never changes.

12. By the word of truth.

13. Meekness.

14. Doers.

15. Hearers.

16. A man looking at himself in a mirror as a metaphor for the believer and God's Word.

17. An unbridled tongue.

18. Visiting widows and orphans in their affliction and keeping oneself unstained from the world.

19. James forbade showing partiality.

20. The poor in the world; they will be heirs of the kingdom.

21. "Love your neighbor as yourself."

22. You are as guilty as if you'd broken all of it.

23. No good.

24. No.

25. Dead.

26. Its works.

27. The demons.

28. Abraham's obedience in offering his son as a sacrifice.

29. Believed.

30. Counted.

31. Righteousness.

32. Rahab the prostitute; she received the messengers (the Israelite spies), and sent them out by another way.

33. Body.

34. Spirit.

35. Faith.

36. Works.

37. Speech.

38. Bits.

39. Horses.

40. Rudders.

41. Ships.

42. Flames.

43. Forests.

44. James said it should not be that people use the same tongue to bless God and curse people.

45. People influenced by God's wisdom have good conduct; they are meek, pure, peaceable, gentle, open to reason, full of mercy and good fruits, impartial, sincere; they make peace; they reap a harvest of righteousness.

46. Bitter jealousy, selfish ambition, disorder, and every vile practice make it evident that a person is not living by God's wisdom.

47. Their inner passions or desires and coveting.

48. Because they put us at enmity with God, who wants us to desire him supremely.

49. Opposes.

50. Gives grace.

51. Submit yourselves.

52. Resist.

53. Draw near.

54. Purify.

55. Cleanse.

56. Humble yourselves.

57. Knowing the right thing to do and failing to do it.

58. Cheating out of their pay those who worked for them.

59. The rich had lived on the earth in luxury and self-indulgence.

60. Murdered.

61. Patient.

62. Steadfast.

63. Job.

64. In the story of Job, we also see the Lord's qualities of compassion and mercy.

65. James told Christians to pray about each other's sicknesses and sins.

66. Christians should confess their sins to each other and pray for each other.

67. They should do all they can to bring back someone who is wandering from the truth.

Acts 12:25–15:35

Acts 12:25–15:35

Acts 12:25–15:35

1. Barnabas and Saul.

2. John Mark.

3. To Cyprus.

4. In the synagogues of the Jews.

5. Bar-Jesus was a magician and a Jewish false prophet.

6. Paul.

7. John Mark left them and returned to Jerusalem.

8. God's choice of Israel and the exodus from Egypt.

9. God's guidance of the Israelites in the wilderness for 40 years.

10. The conquest of the Promised Land under Joshua.

11. The Old Testament judges; Samuel.

12. King Saul.

13. King David.

14. The promise of a Savior from David's offspring.

15. The Jews were of the family of Abraham.

16. The fulfillment, by Jesus' death, of promises concerning the Messiah.

17. Prophecies about Christ from the Psalms.

18. The Law of Moses.

19. The Prophets.

20. A warning quoted from Habakkuk.

21. Good news.

22. By raising Jesus.

23. Forgiveness of sins.

24. All that the Law of Moses could not free them from.

25. Almost the whole city.

26. They were filled with jealousy and began to contradict what Paul said, reviling him.

27. Gentiles.

28. The ends of the earth.

29. As many Gentiles as were appointed to eternal life believed.

30. It was spreading throughout the whole region.

31. The Jews stirred up persecution against Paul and Barnabas and drove them out of their district.

32. Joy and the Holy Spirit.

33. Believed.

34. Stirred up the Gentiles and poisoned their minds against the Christians.

35. Because enemies planned to mistreat and stone them.

36. Continued to preach the gospel.

37. They thought that he and Barnabas were gods; they called Barnabas Zeus and Paul Hermes.

38. They persuaded the crowds, stoned Paul, dragged him out of the city, and left him for dead.

39. They preached the gospel, making many disciples.

40. They strengthened the souls of the disciples and encouraged them to continue in the faith.

41. We must enter through many tribulations.

42. Elders.

43. A door of faith to the Gentiles.

44. The men who came to Antioch were from Judea. They taught: "Unless you are circumcised according to the law of Moses, you cannot be saved."

45. Paul and Barnabas.

46. The church decided to send men to Jerusalem to ask the apostles and the elders there to decide the issue.

47. The conversion of the Gentiles.

48. It was necessary to circumcise Gentiles and to order them to keep the law of Moses.

49. People were very divided, because it says, "after there had been much debate."

50. Hear the word of the gospel and believe.

51. God showed the genuineness of the Gentiles' faith by giving them the Holy Spirit.

52. None..

53. Peter said these Jews were trying to put a yoke on the Gentiles which they—the Jews—and their fathers had not been able to bear.

54. The grace of the Lord Jesus.

55. Paul and Barnabas related the signs and wonders God had done among the Gentiles through them.

56. James.

57. Amos.

58. Not.

59. The Holy Spirit.

60. Us.

61. To Antioch.

Paul's Epistle to the Galatians

Galatians 1–6

Galatians 1–6

1. Give thanks to God.

2. Work of faith.

3. Labor of love.

4. Steadfastness of hope.

5. Give thanks to God.

6. Faith.

7. Growing abundantly.

8. Love.

9. Increasing.

10. Thank God.

11. Faith in Christ Jesus

12. Love.

13. Thank my God.

14. Joy.

15. Partnership in the gospel.

16. Give thanks to my God.

17. The grace of God.

18. Enriched in him.

19. Speech.

20. Knowledge.

21. In every other opening, Paul gives thanks for the people he's writing to and for something about them. He does not do that in Galatians.

22. Astonished.

23. Deserting.

24. Turning to another gospel.

25. "Let him be accursed."

26. Paul had not received the gospel from any man.

27. Paul received the gospel through a revelation of Jesus Christ.

28. Before receiving the gospel, Paul persecuted the church of God violently, trying to destroy it.

29. Paul consulted with no one.

30. Paul set before the original apostles the gospel that he proclaimed to the Gentiles.

31. The apostles' response was to recognize the grace of God given to Paul and to give him the right hand of fellowship.

32. Paul rebuked Cephas (or Peter).

33. Because their conduct was not in step with the truth of the gospel.

34. Works of the law.

35. Faith in Jesus Christ.

36. Believed in Christ Jesus.

37. Faith in Christ.

38. Works of the law.

39. Works of the law.

40. Justified.

41. Those of faith.

42. Justify.

43. By faith.

44. Preached the gospel.

45. Faith.

46. Under a curse.

47. All things written.

48. Do.

49. By becoming a curse for them.

50. The blessing of Abraham.

51. Faith.

52. Our guardian.

53. God's purpose was always that we (his people) might be justified by faith.

54. Sons of God.

55. Faith.

56. They had been enslaved to other gods—which aren't even gods.

57. Turn back again.

58. The Galatians had not scorned or despised him, but had received him as an angel of God, as Christ Jesus.

59. The Galatians would have gouged out their eyes and given them to Paul.

60. Anguish.

61. His little children.

62. They would be obligated to keep the whole law.

63. Severed from Christ.

64. Fallen away from grace.

65. Freedom.

66. An opportunity for the flesh.

67. Through love, they are to serve one another.

68. By walking by the Spirit.

69. The desires of the flesh will be against the desires of the Spirit.

70. Love, joy, peace, patience, kindness, goodness, faithfulness, gentleness, self-control.

71. The cross of Christ.

72. A new creation.

Acts 15:36–18:18

Acts
15:36–18:18

Acts 15:36–18:18

1. John Mark.

2. Because he had withdrawn from (or deserted) them on their last missionary journey together.

3. They disagreed so sharply that they separated.

4. Cyprus.

5. Silas.

6. Syria and Cilicia.

7. Paul picked up Timothy, who had a Jewish mother and a Greek father.

8. The decisions from the Jerusalem Council to the churches.

9. "So the churches were strengthened in the faith, and they increased in numbers daily."

10. Paul and his companions didn't go to Bithynia because the Spirit of Jesus did not allow them to do so.

11. A man calling, "Come over to Macedonia and help us."

12. God had called them to preach the gospel to them.

13. In Philippi, Paul and his companions went to the riverside, because they supposed there would be a place of prayer there.

14. Lydia was a seller of purple goods. The Lord opened her heart to pay attention to what was said by Paul.

15. Paul cast out the spirit from the slave girl.

16. Because they had lost their hope of gain from her.

17. They were thrown into prison, and their feet were fastened in the stocks.

18. They were praying and singing hymns to God.

19. A great earthquake caused the doors to open and the bonds to become unfastened; the jailer drew his sword to kill himself.

20. "What must I do to be saved?"

21. "Believe in the Lord Jesus and you will be saved, you and your household."

22. Yes.

23. Thessalonica.

24. Luke stayed behind in Philippi; he no longer says "we" when describing Paul's travels.

25. Some of the Jews, many of the devout Greeks, and not a few leading women were persuaded and joined Paul and Silas.

26. They accused the Christians of turning the world upside down, acting against the decrees of Caesar, and having another king, Jesus.

27. Berea.

28. Received.

29. Eagerness.

30. Examining the Scriptures.

31. Paul went on to Athens, while Silas and Timothy stayed in Berea.

32. The idols that filled Athens.

33. To the Aeropagus.

34. Paul said he proclaimed to them what they worshiped as unknown.

35. God would one day judge the world in righteousness.

36. God commanded all men everywhere to repent.

37. Some mocked; others said they would hear him again; and some joined him and believed.

38. Corinth.

39. Aquila and Priscilla.

40. They were tentmakers.

41. Paul reasoned in the synagogue every Sabbath, trying to persuade Jews and Greeks.

42. They opposed and reviled him.

43. To the Gentiles.

44. He believed in the Lord, with his entire household.

45. Because he had many in Corinth who were his people; they needed to hear the gospel so they could believe.

46. For a year and a half.

Paul's First Epistle to the Thessalonians

1. He was sent away for his safety because of angry Jews.

2. They had dragged Jason and several of the brothers before the authorities and took money from them before letting them go.

3. Angry Jews from Thessalonica had come to Berea to stir up the crowds.

4. Paul sent Timothy to find out about the Thessalonians when he could stand it no longer.

I Thessalonians 1–5

1. Work.

2. Labor.

3. Steadfastness.

4. Chosen them.

5. Word.

6. Power.

7. The Holy Spirit.

8. Full conviction.

9. Imitators.

10. The Lord.

11. The word.

12. Much affliction.

13. Joy of the Holy Spirit.

14. Examples.

15. Faith in God.

16. Everywhere.

17. God.

18. Idols.

19. Living and true God.

20. His Son.

21. He and his companions had been shamefully treated in Philippi.

22. Boldness.

23. Much conflict.

24. Paul's goal when he spoke was to please God.

25. Gentle.

26. Nursing mother.

27. Her own children.

28. Their own selves.

29. So they wouldn't be a burden to them.

30. Paul's conduct among the Thessalonians had been holy and righteous and blameless.

31. Father.

32. Children.

33. Exhorted.

34. Encouraged.

35. Charged.

36. Walk in a manner worthy.

37. The Thessalonians had accepted the gospel, not as the word of men, but as the word of God.

38. In suffering for Christ.

39. Moved.

40. Afflictions.

41. Destined.

42. Increase and abound in love.

43. Establish.

44. Blameless.

45. Holiness.

46. Do so more and more.

47. Sanctification.

48. Abstain.

49. Control.

50. Holiness.

51. Honor.

52. Know God.

53. Love each other more and more.

54. Quietly.

55. Mind their own affairs.

56. With their hands.

57. Grieve.

58. Hope.

59. When the Lord returns, he will bring with him Christians who have died.

60. All believers will be with the Lord forever.

61. To use these words to encourage one another.

62. The day of the Lord.

63. No one knows exactly when Christ would return; it will be unexpected.

64. It should not surprise Christians, like the coming of a thief.

65. They should be sober, having put on the breastplate of faith and love, and having, as a helmet, the hope of salvation.

66. Wrath.

67. Salvation.

68. His people would live with him.

69. They should encourage one another.

70. Labor among them.

71. Admonishing.

72. Encouraging.

73. Helping.

74. Patient.

75. Evil for evil.

76. Rejoice.

77. Without ceasing.

78. Everything.

79. Completely.

80. Blameless.

81. Faithful.

82. Surely do it.

Paul's Second Epistle to the Thessalonians

2 Thessalonians 1–3

1. No.

2. Paul commented on their steadfastness and faith in all the persecutions and afflictions they "are enduring" (v.4); he said they were suffering for the kingdom of God (v.5); he described the Lord's return as the time when the persecuted Christians will have relief and their persecutors will be punished (vv. 6-10).

3. He will take vengeance on those who do not know God and who do not obey the gospel of the Lord Jesus.

4. His saints.

5. The Thessalonians had been told that the day of the Lord had already come.

6. The rebellion would come first and the man of lawlessness would be revealed.

7. Opposes.

8. Exalts himself.

9. God

10. The breath of the Lord Jesus' mouth.

11. Bring the lawless one to nothing.

12. Because they refuse to love the truth.

13. Delusion.

14. What is false.

15. Beloved.

16. Chose.

17. Stand firm.

18. Hold to the traditions they had been taught.

19. Idleness.

20. Work.

21. The Thessalonians should imitate Paul and his companions.

22. Idle.

23. Paying for it.

24. Burden.

25. Set an example.

26. Unwilling to work.

27. Eat.

28. Do their work.

29. Earn their own living.

30. The rest of the church was to keep away from any brother walking in idleness.

31. Weary in doing good.

32. The other believers should have nothing to do with the person who wouldn't obey.

33. An enemy.

34. A brother.

Acts
18:18–19:20

Acts 18:18–19:20

1. Aquila and Priscilla left Corinth with Paul; he left them in Ephesus.

2. Antioch.

3. Phrygia.

4. Galatia.

5. Paul went back through the churches he had planted earlier, strengthening all the disciples.

6. Three months.

7. Reasoning.

8. Persuading.

9. Reason.

10. Two years.

11. The seven brothers were attacked and overpowered by the demon-possessed man, so that they fled the house naked and wounded.

12. As a result, fear fell upon the people in the area and they extolled the name of Jesus.

13. They brought their magic books together and burned them.

14. So the word of the Lord continued to increase and prevail mightily.

Acts Review: Acts 1:1–19:20

1. Luke wrote Acts.

2. The Gospel According to Luke was part 1.

3. Acts is about what Jesus continued to do and teach, through the apostles by the Holy Spirit.

4. Jesus promised his disciples that they would receive power when the Holy Spirit came upon them.

5. Jesus told the disciples to be his witnesses, in Jerusalem, and in all Judea and Samaria, and to the end of the earth.

6. The basic outline of Acts shows how this occurred: the Holy Spirit came, Jesus' disciples witnessed about him, first in Jerusalem, then in the rest of Judea and in Samaria, and then in the rest of the world.

7. The Holy Spirit came to live in believers.

8. This occurred on the day of Pentecost (or firstfruits).

9. Disciples saw tongues of fire on each of them, heard the sound of a great wind, and spoke to people in languages they had not learned.

10. Peter preached a sermon.

11. This was surprising because, earlier, Peter had been afraid to even admit he knew Jesus.

12. The Holy Spirit in Peter made the difference in his boldness.

13. The people who had shouted, "Crucify him," about Jesus were cut to the heart and asked what they should do.

14. The Holy Spirit had convicted these people.

15. 3,000 people were converted.

16. Peter and John said they had to obey God rather than man.

17. The sin of Ananias and Sapphira was in lying about how much they had given. They were struck dead.

18. The church in Jerusalem gave the seven men the job of fairly distributing food to the widows.

19. "A great many of the priests became obedient to the faith."

20. The first Christian martyr was Stephen.

21. His murder and the persecution that came after caused the Christians to leave Jerusalem, and they took the gospel everywhere they went.

22. Saul watched Stephen's stoning and went on to persecute Christians.

23. Philip proclaimed the gospel to Samaritans and to an Ethiopian man.

24. Saul, on his way to Damascus to further persecute Christians, saw a bright light that blinded him and heard the voice of Jesus. Three days later, a believer named Ananias prayed for him to receive his sight, and he was baptized.

25. The centurion was Cornelius.

26. Peter saw unclean animals being lowered from heaven and heard a voice saying, "Kill and eat," and then "What God has made clean, do not call common."

27. While Peter preached the gospel to Cornelius, the Holy Spirit fell on the Gentiles who listened.

28. Believers were first called Christians at Antioch.

29. Barnabas brought Saul to help with the teaching at Antioch.

30. Herod had James executed.

31. Herod planned to execute Peter next.

32. Christians in Jerusalem prayed for Peter while he was in jail.

33. An angel released Peter from jail, while doors, gates, and chains opened by themselves and no guards saw Peter and the angel leave.

34. An angel of the Lord struck Herod; he was eaten by worms and died.

35. Believers at Antioch were praying, and the Holy Spirit told them to set apart Saul and Barnabas for work he had for them.

36. Whenever Paul went to a new city, he preached in the Jewish synagogue first.

37. Paul (and Peter) used Old Testament Scripture when preaching to Jews.

38. Peter is considered the apostle to the Jews and Paul is the apostle to the Gentiles.

39. In Lystra, Paul was first worshiped as a god, then stoned and left for dead.

40. Men from Judea were teaching that Gentiles had to be circumcised to be saved.

41. The church at Antioch sent a message to the apostles and elders in Jerusalem to settle this debate.

42. The Jerusalem Council decided that the Gentiles did not need to be circumcised to be saved; salvation is by the grace of God alone.

43. Paul and Barnabas separated because Barnabas wanted to take John Mark on their next missionary journey, but Paul did not want to take him since he had deserted them before.

44. Yes, they were reconciled and Paul came to find John Mark to be very helpful in later ministry.

45. Timothy joined Paul.

46. Europe.

47. Paul and Silas were beaten, and then were put into stocks in prison.

48. Paul left Thessalonica abruptly because of angry mobs and persecution.

49. Paul preached at the Areopagus (or Mars Hill).

50. Paul lived with Aquila and Priscilla; all three of them were tentmakers.

More Acts Review: The Gospel's Progress

E. The gospel moved to Gentiles in Asia, and what to do about Gentile Christians was decided.

6. The Jerusalem Council was held, to determine whether or not Gentile Christians had to be circumcised to receive salvation.

1. Barnabas got Saul (Paul) from Tarsus and brought him to the church at Antioch, where they spent some time teaching the Christians there.

5. Paul and Barnabas got into a debate with some Jewish Christians in Antioch.

3. People in Lystra tried to offer sacrifices to Paul and Barnabas, thinking they were gods.

4. Paul was stoned and left for dead.

2. The Holy Spirit told the church in Antioch to separate Paul and Barnabas out for work he had for them to do.

7. Paul and Barnabas got into a dispute over whether or not John Mark could go with them on their next missionary journey.

B. The apostles boldly proclaimed the gospel in Jerusalem.

5. Seven men were appointed to make sure food distribution to the widows was fair.

4. Ananias and Sapphira lied to the Holy Spirit.

2. Peter preached a bold sermon in which 3,000 people believed.

3. Peter and John healed a lame man, preached a sermon, and were told never to speak about Jesus again.

1. The Holy Spirit came to dwell in every believer, with visible signs of flames, and with the sound of a great wind.

A. Jesus told his disciples that they would receive power from the Holy Spirit to be his witnesses in Jerusalem, in Samaria and all Judea, and to the uttermost parts of the earth.

D. The gospel made its first move to the Gentiles.

6. King Herod enjoyed praise as a god and was eaten by worms and died.

5. An angel released Peter from prison.

2. Peter preached to Cornelius, a Roman centurion.

4. James, the brother of John, was put to death to please the Jews.

1. Peter saw a vision of unclean animals and heard a voice telling him to kill and eat.

3. The Holy Spirit fell upon Gentiles as they listened to the gospel.

F. The gospel moved from Asia to Europe.

5. Paul spent three years teaching, reasoning, and persuading in Ephesus.

4. Paul went alone to Athens, where he spoke of Christ on Mars Hill.

2. After casting a demon out of a slave girl in Philippi, Paul and Silas were imprisoned, but an earthquake freed them, and their jailer believed in Christ.

1. The Holy Spirit made it clear to Paul that he was not to go on to Asia, but to cross over into Macedonia with the gospel.

3. Paul stayed for a little while in Thessalonica, but angry mobs ran him out.

C. The gospel moved into the rest of Judea and Samaria.

2. A great persecution arose against the Christians.

3. Philip, after sharing the gospel in Samaria, explained it to an Ethiopian man riding in a chariot.

4. Saul, after persecuting Christians diligently, was converted to faith in Christ.

1. Stephen was stoned to death by angry Jews.

Paul's First Epistle to the Corinthians

1. Ephesus.

1 Corinthians 1–6

1. Quarreling and divisions in the church.
2. United.
3. Mind.
4. Judgment.
5. Christ had sent Paul to preach the gospel.
6. The power of gospel preaching isn't in words of eloquent wisdom, but in the cross of Christ.
7. Jews demanded signs.
8. Greeks sought wisdom.
9. Paul preached Christ crucified.
10. That was a stumbling block to Jews.
11. It was folly to Gentiles.
12. To those whom God has called, Christ is the power of God and the wisdom of God.
13. Boast.
14. Christ has become to his people wisdom, righteousness, sanctification, and redemption.
15. God's people can only boast in the Lord.
16. Paul deliberately did not use lofty speech or wisdom.
17. Jesus Christ and him crucified.
18. The wisdom of men.
19. The power of God.
20. When people understand God's wisdom, it is because God has revealed it to them through the Spirit.
21. So they can understand the things freely given to them by God.
22. Accept.
23. Folly.
24. Is not able to.
25. Jealousy.

26. Strife.

27. Human.

28. Human ministers are servants.

29. God.

30. Folly with God.

31. Boast in men.

32. Sexual immorality.

33. His father's wife.

34. Pagans.

35. Arrogant.

36. Paul said they should mourn over this instead, and should remove the immoral person from among them.

37. Sexual immorality.

38. Christ.

39. A temple of the Holy Spirit.

40. Bought.

41. Price.

42. Glorify God.

43. Christians were getting upset with each other and taking each other to court.

44. Paul said it would be better for Christians to suffer wrong or be defrauded by another Christian than to take that person to court before unbelievers.

1 Corinthians 7–16

1 Corinthians
7–16

1. Food offered to idols.

2. A stumbling block.

3. Your brothers.

4. Christ.

5. His brother stumble.

6. His own.

7. Free.

8. Servant.

9. Win.

10. Let no one seek his own good, but the good of his neighbor.

11. Whether you eat or drink, or whatever you do, do all to the glory of God.

12. The human body.

13. One.

14. Many.

15. Hand.

16. "I have no need of you."

17. God arranges the members in the body as he chose.

18. If one member of the body suffers, all suffer together.

19. If one member is honored, all rejoice together.

20. Nothing.

21. Patient.

22. Kind.

23. Envy.

24. Boast.

25. Arrogant.

26. Rude.

27. Its own way.

28. Irritable.

29. Resentful.

30. The truth.

31. Bears.

32. Believes.

33. Hopes.

34. Endures.

35. Ends.

36. Some in Corinth were saying that there was no resurrection of the dead.

37. Christ.

38. Futile.

39. In their sins.

40. Christians who have died have perished.

41. They are more to be pitied than anyone else.

42. Christ has been raised from the dead.

43. Death will be destroyed.

44. Changed.

45. A Christian's body is perishable when it dies.

46. Christians' bodies will be raised imperishable.

47. Dishonor.

48. Glory.

49. Weakness.

50. Power.

51. The bodies of Christians still alive when Jesus returns will be changed.

52. The dead will be raised imperishable.

53. Moment.

54. Twinkling of an eye.

55. Death will be swallowed up in victory.

56. Steadfast.

57. Immovable.

58. The work of the Lord.

59. In vain.

Paul's Second Epistle to the Corinthians

2 Corinthians 1–7

2 Corinthians 1–7

1. Affliction.

2. Anguish.

3. Many tears.

4. Pain.

5. Abundant love.

6. God comforted the downcast Paul with Titus's coming.

7. Longing.

8. Mourning.

9. Zeal.

10. Regret.

11. Repenting.

12. Godly.

13. Forgive.

14. Comfort.

15. Reaffirm.

16. Love.

2 Corinthians 8–13

1. Decided in his heart.
2. Reluctantly.
3. Compulsion.
4. Sparingly.
5. Bountifully.
6. Bountifully.
7. Cheerful.
8. Sufficiency.
9. Things.
10. Times.
11. Generous.
12. Many thanksgivings.
13. Rich.
14. Poor.
15. Poverty.
16. Rich.
17. Inexpressible
18. Labors.
19. Imprisonments.
20. Beatings.
21. Death.
22. Five.
23. Rods.
24. Stoned.
25. Shipwrecked.
26. A night and a day.
27. Journeys.
28. Rivers.
29. Robbers.
30. Gentiles.
31. City.
32. Wilderness.
33. Sea.
34. False.
35. Toil.
36. Hardship.
37. Sleepless.
38. Hunger.
39. Thirst.
40. Cold.
41. Exposure.
42. Anxiety.
43. Churches.
44. Three times.
45. Grace.
46. Perfect.
47. Weakness.
48. Weaknesses.
49. Power of Christ.
50. Weaknesses.
51. Insults.
52. Hardships.
53. Persecutions.
54. Calamities.
55. Strong.

Acts 19:21–20:38

Acts 19:21–20:38

1. Demetrius was a silversmith, upset because Paul taught that gods made with hands (like Artemis) are not really gods. Not only might Artemis not receive the honor she deserved, but the silversmiths wouldn't earn as much money.

2. To Macedonia.

3. To Greece; three months.

4. Paul's sermon continued until midnight.

5. Eutychus was sitting in the window.

6. Eutychus fell asleep and fell out of the window.

7. Eutychus was taken up dead, but Paul restored him to life.

8. Paul continued speaking with the believers until daybreak.

9. Jerusalem.

10. The elders of Ephesus.

11. Paul said the Holy Spirit testified to him that imprisonment and afflictions awaited him in Jerusalem.

Paul's Epistle to the Romans

Romans 1–5

Romans 1–5

1. God.

2. His prophets.

3. Holy Scriptures.

4. His Son.

5. David.

6. Flesh.

7. The Son of God.

8. Resurrection from the dead.

9. Jesus Christ our Lord.

10. All the nations.

11. Obedience.

12. Faith

13. Salvation.

14. Believes.

15. Jew.

16. Gentile.

17. Righteousness.

18. Revealed.

19. Faith.

20. Faith.

21. Wrath of God.

22. All ungodliness and unrighteousness.

23. Eternal power and divine nature.

24. Suppress it.

25. Excuse.

26. Futile.

27. They have become darkened.

28. Fools.

29. Exchanged the glory.

30. Immortal God.

31. Images.

32. Debased mind.

33. What ought not to be done.

34. The hearers of the law.

35. Righteous.

36. Doers of the law.

37. Justified.

38. No, not at all.

39. Under sin.

40. None.

41. One.

42. Seeks.

43. All.

44. Good.

45. Mouth.

46. Accountable.

47. Human being.

48. Justified.

49. The righteousness of God has been mani-fested.

50. The law.

51. The Law and the Prophets witnessed to this righteousness.

52. Faith.

53. Jesus Christ.

54. Believe.

55. Distinction.

56. Sinned.

57. Fall short.

58. God's grace.

59. Gift

60. Redemption.

61. Propitiation.

62. Blood.

63. Just.

64. Justifier.

65. By faith.

66. Works of the law.

67. Abraham and David.

68. "Abraham believed God, and it was counted to him as righteousness."

69. Count.

70. Sin.

71. Our sake.

72. Believe.

73. Raised from the dead Jesus our Lord.

74. Trespasses.

75. Justification.

76. Justified by faith.

77. Peace.

78. God.

79. Access.

80. Grace.

81. Hope.

82. Glory.

83. Sufferings

84. Endurance.

85. Character.

86. Hope.

87. He gave his Son while they were still sinners.

88. Enemies.

89. Reconciled.

90. Rejoice.

91. Adam and Christ.

92. Sin came into the world through Adam, and so death spread to all men.

93. Grace.

94. Righteousness.

95. Life.

96. Disobedience.

97. Sinners.

98. Obedience.

99. Righteous.

Romans 6-8

Romans 6–8

1. Sin.
2. Grace.
3. Sin.
4. Law.
5. Grace.
6. United.
7. Crucified.
8. Dead.
9. Live.
10. To God.
11. Alive.
12. Reign
13. Obey.
14. Instruments of unrighteousness.
15. God.
16. Death.
17. Life.
18. Instruments of righteousness.
19. The Roman Christians were once slaves of sin.
20. They had been set free from sin.
21. Obedient.
22. Heart.
23. Sinful passions.
24. Death.
25. Holy.
26. Righteous.
27. Good.
28. The very thing he hated.
29. Sin.
30. The law of God.
31. Captive.
32. Condemnation.
33. The flesh.
34. The Spirit.
35. Put to death.
36. Children.
37. God.
38. Fellow heirs.
39. Sufferings.
40. Glory.
41. Creation.
42. Helps.
43. Weakness.
44. Good.
45. Called.
46. Justified.
47. Glorified.
48. Killed.
49. Nothing.

Romans 9–11

Romans 9–11

1. Flesh.
2. Promise.
3. God chose Jacob but did not choose Esau.
4. Not yet born.
5. Nothing either good or bad.
6. Injustice.

7. Human will.

8. Exertion.

9. God who has mercy.

10. Pharoah.

11. Find fault.

12. Resist his will.

13. Man.

14. God.

15. A potter and the pots he makes, for whatever uses he chooses.

16. Faith.

17. Righteousness.

18. Their own.

19. Remnant.

20. By grace.

21. Hardened.

22. Salvation.

23. Jews.

24. Gentiles.

25. Proud.

26. Unbelief.

27. Faith.

28. Continue in their unbelief.

29. Wisdom.

30. Knowledge.

31. Unsearchable.

32. Inscrutable.

33. The mind of the Lord.

34. Counselor.

Romans 12–16

1. Present.

2. Living sacrifice.

3. Conformed.

4. Transformed.

5. Minds.

6. Highly.

7. Members.

8. One.

9. Function.

10. Differ.

11. Use.

12. Genuine.

13. Honor.

14. Contributing.

15. Hospitality.

16. Rejoicing.

17. Weeping.

18. Harmony.

19. Haughty.

20. Lowly.

21. Hope.

22. Tribulation.

23. Prayer.

24. Repay.

25. Evil.

26. Evil.

27. Evil.

28. Good.

29. Honorable.

30. Peaceably.

31. All.

32. Subject.

33. Instituted.

34. God has appointed.

35. You shall love your neighbor as yourself.

36. Love will not do wrong to a neighbor.

37. The law.

38. Properly.

39. Lord Jesus Christ.

40. The flesh.

41. Eat.

42. Days.

43. Fully convinced in his own mind.

44. Pass judgment.

45. Honor of the Lord.

46. Stumbling block.

47. Hindrance.

48. Christ.

49. Build him up.

50. Please.

51. Harmony.

52. One Voice.

53. Glory of God.

54. Servant.

55. The Gentiles.

56. All nations.

57. Obedience.

58. Faith.

59. Wise God.

60. Glory.

Acts 21–28

Acts
21–28

Acts 21–28

1. They would bind Paul and hand him over to the Gentiles.

2. Imprisoned.

3. Die.

4. People.

5. Law.

6. Greeks.

7. The Roman tribune saved Paul.

8. Carried.

9. Soldiers.

10. Far away to the Gentiles.

11. By pointing out that he was a Roman citizen, because it was illegal to flog a Roman citizen who had not yet been found guilty.

12. The hope and the resurrection of the dead.

13. The result was a violent argument between the Pharisees and the Sadducees.

14. The tribune feared Paul would be torn in pieces.

15. Jesus.

16. In Rome.

17. Paul's enemies vowed to neither eat nor drink until they had killed him; there were more than forty of them.

18. Paul's nephew heard of the plot.

19. The tribune sent Paul to Caesarea.

20. Paul's protection consisted of 200 soldiers, with 70 horsemen and 200 spearmen.

21. Felix.

22. Paul was reasoning with Felix about righteousness, self-control, and the coming judgment.

23. Money.

24. Two years.

25. Kill Paul.

26. Caesar.

27. Prophets.

28. Moses.

29. Suffer.

30. Rise from the dead.

31. The Jews ("our people").

32. The Gentiles.

33. Deserve death or imprisonment.

34. Set free.

35. They didn't see the sun or stars for many days.

36. They abandoned all hope of being saved.

37. Luke was with them because the author speaks of hope of "our being saved."

38. The angel said they would lose the ship, but no lives.

39. Fourteen days.

40. Kill the prisoners to keep them from escaping.

41. All of them

42. A snake fastened on Paul's hand but he suffered no harm.

43. Paul healed the island chief's father of fever and dysentery.

44. In Rome, Paul stayed by himself with a soldier to guard him.

45. The Jews.

46. The Law of Moses.

47. The Prophets.

48. Two years.

49. The kingdom of God.

50. All boldness.

51. Without hindrance.

More Acts Review

Places

1. Jerusalem, all Judea and Samaria, and to the end of the earth.

2. Antioch.

3. Jerusalem.

4. Ethiopia.

5. Europe (Macedonia).

6. Jerusalem.

7. Rome.

8. Ephesus.

People

1. Stephen.

2. Peter.

3. Paul.

4. King Herod.

5. Peter.

6. James.

7. Barnabas.

8. Timothy.

9. John Mark.

The Book

1. Acts is the description of how Jesus' command was carried out.

2. Luke; The Gospel According to Luke.

3. Paul lived by himself in a house, but under guard, and people came to him. He preached the gospel to them boldly and without hindrance.

Miscellaneous

1. The Holy Spirit.

2. Visible: tongues of fire; audible: the sound of a great wind and Christians speaking to others in languages they had never learned.

3. Christians fled Jerusalem because of the persecution that began when Stephen was stoned, and everywhere they went, they took the gospel.

4. Hardships faced by Paul: many imprisonments; countless beatings; being often near death; thirty-nine lashes five different times; beaten with rods three times; stoned; shipwrecked three times, once being adrift at sea for a day and a night; dangers from rivers, from robbers, from the Jews, from Gentiles, from dangers in the city, from dangers in the wilderness, from dangers at sea, and from dangers from false brothers; toil and hardship; many a sleepless night; hunger and thirst; cold and exposure; daily pressure of anxiety for all the churches.

Epistle Review: Part 1

1. Galatians

2. 1–2 Thessalonians

3. Romans

4. James

5. 1–2 Corinthians

Paul's Epistle to the Ephesians

1. Paul was a prisoner when he wrote Ephesians.

Ephesians 1–3

Ephesians 1–3

1. Choosing.

2. Predestining.

3. Spiritual blessing.

4. His will.

5. His glorious grace.

6. His grace.

7. Unite.

8. Heaven.

9. Earth.

10. The counsel of his will.

11. In Christ.

12. Blood.

13. Forgiveness.

14. Sealed.

15. Guarantee.

16. Hope.

17. Glorious inheritance.

18. His power.

19. Rule.

20. Authority.

21. Power.

22. Dominion.

23. Name.

24. The one to come.

25. All things.

26. All things.

27. The church.

28. Body.

29. Fullness.

30. Dead.

31. This world.

32. Passions.

33. Children of wrath.

34. But God.

35. Alive.

36. Christ.

37. Raised us up.

38. Seated us.

39. The great love with which he loved us.

40. Mercy.

41. Grace.

42. Faith.

43. Doing.

44. Gift.

45. Works.

46. Separated.

47. Strangers.

48. No hope.

49. God.

50. The blood of Christ.

51. God.

52. One body.

53. The cross.

54. Hostility.

55. Access in one Spirit to the Father.

56. Fellow citizens.

57. The household of God.

58. God.

59. Apostles and prophets.

60. Cornerstone.

Ephesians 4–6

Ephesians 4–6

1. Paul urged the Ephesians to walk in a manner worthy of the calling to which they had been called.

2. Paul encouraged them to maintain the unity of the Spirit in the bond of peace.

3. 4:25   falsehood   speaking the truth

4. 4:28   stealing   labor and sharing

5. 4:29   corrupting talk   talk that builds up

6. 4:31-5:2   bitterness, wrath, anger clamor, slander, malice   kindness, tenderheartedness, forgiveness, love

7. 5:3-4   sexual immorality, impurity, covetousness, filthiness, foolish talk, crude joking   thanksgiving for God's good gifts

8. 5:18   drunkenness   being filled with the Holy Spirit

9. Husband and wife.

10. Christ gave himself up for the church.

11. Sanctify.

12. Spot.

13. Wrinkle.

14. Holy.

15. Without blemish.

16. Submit to.

17. The church.

18. Christ.

19. Truth.

20. Righteousness.

21. The readiness given by the gospel.

22. Faith.

23. Salvation.

24. The word of God.

25. Praying.

Paul's Epistle to the Colossians

Colossians 1-2

Colossians 1–2

1. Epaphras.

2. Hearing about the Colossians' faith in Christ Jesus and their love for all the saints.

3. God's will.

4. Worthy of the Lord.

5. Every good work.

6. The knowledge of God.

7. God's beloved Son.

8. Redemption.

9. Forgiveness of sins.

10. Image of the invisible God.

11. Firstborn of all creation.

12. By him.

13. Created.

14. Through.

15. For.

16. Before all things.

17. All things hold together.

18. Head of the body, the church.

19. The beginning.

20. Firstborn from the dead.

21. Preeminent.

22. All the fullness of God was pleased to dwell.

23. Reconciles.

24. All things.

25. Peace.

26. The blood of his cross.

27. Reconciled

28. Body of flesh.

29. His death.

30. Holy.

31. Blameless.

32. Above reproach.

33. God's mystery.

34. All the treasures of wisdom and knowledge.

35. Deity.

36. Bodily.

37. Filled.

38. All rule and authority.

39. Body of flesh.

40. Baptism.

41. Alive.

42. Forgiven.

43. Canceled.

44. Disarmed.

45. Shame.

46. Triumphing.

47. Christ.

48. Hope of glory.

49. The full assurance of understanding and the knowledge of God's mystery, which is Christ.

50. Continue.

51. Shifting.

52. Gospel.

53. Received.

54. In him.

55. Established.

56. Takes you captive.

57. Christ.

58. Pass judgment.

59. These things were just the shadow of things to come; the substance was Christ.

60. Hold fast.

61. Asceticism.

62. Angels.

63. Visions.

Colossians 3–4

Colossians 3–4

1. The things that are above.

2. On things above, not on things on the earth.

3. Christians have put off the old self with its evil practices, and have put on the new self.

4. Paul told the Colossians to put to death or to put away: sexual immorality, impurity, passion, evil desire, covetousness, anger, wrath, malice, slander, obscene talk, lying.

5. Paul told Christians to put on: compassionate hearts, kindness, humility, meekness, patience, forgiveness, love.

6. Sent Tychichus to the Colossians with this letter; Onesimus went with him.

7. The Colossians were to have this letter read in the church of the Laodiceans.

8. The Colossians were to read the letter Paul had sent to Laodicea.

Paul's Epistle to Philemon

Philemon

Philemon

1. No.

2. Paul asked Philemon to receive Onesimus as he would have received Paul himself.

3. Paul asked Philemon to charge anything Onesimus owed him to Paul's account.

4. Commanded.

5. Appeal.

6. Love's.

7. Old man.

8. Prisoner.

9. Child.

10. Heart.

11. Serve.

12. Imprisonment.

13. Consent.

14. Accord.

15. Compulsion.

16. A beloved brother.

17. Repay.

18. His own self.

19. Confident.

20. Obedience.

21. Even more.

Paul's Epistle to the Philippians

1. Caesar's household.

Philippians 1–4

Philippians 1–4

1. The Philippians' partnership in the gospel.

2. The Philippians were partners with Paul in giving and receiving.

3. They had sent gifts—money—as help for Paul's needs.

4. Paul had learned to be content, whatever his situation.

5. Because he could do all things through Christ who strengthened him.

6. Paul rejoiced that Christ was being proclaimed.

7. Paul's imprisonment had served to advance the gospel.

8. Paul specifically mentioned the whole imperial guard.

9. Life and death.

10. Christ.

11. Living on in the flesh meant fruitful labor for Paul.

12. Gain.

13. If he "departed" (died), Paul would be with Christ, and that was far better.

14. Progress.

15. Joy.

16. If the Philippian Christians would be of the same mind, having the same love, being in full accord and of one mind.

17. As more significant than themselves.

18. The interests of others.

19. Christ Jesus.

20. Equality with God.

21. Made himself nothing, taking the form of a servant.

22. Christ became obedient to the point of death, even death on a cross.

23. God highly exalted him and bestowed on him a name above every name.

24. Every knee shall bow and every tongue shall confess that Jesus is Lord.

25. Even though Paul might die for his faith, he was glad and rejoiced.

26. Be glad and rejoice with him.

27. Epaphroditus had been near death.

28. So the Philippians might rejoice when they saw him again.

29. Rubbish.

30. Knowing Christ Jesus his Lord.

31. Righteousness.

32. The law.

33. In Christ.

34. Faith in Christ.

35. Christ.

36. His resurrection.

37. His sufferings.

38. Imitate him.

39. The many people who did not imitate him in this, but who were Christ's enemies.

40. Brothers and his joy and crown.

41. Rejoice in the Lord always.

42. Anxious about anything.

43. Prayer.

44. Supplication.

45. Thanksgiving.

46. Requests be made known to God.

47. The peace of God would guard their hearts and minds.

Paul's First Epistle to Timothy and Paul's Epistle to Titus

1 Timothy and Titus

I Timothy and Titus

1. Paul had left Timothy in Ephesus and had gone on to Macedonia.

2. Teach any different doctrine.

3. Paul had left Titus in Crete to "put what remained into order" (to organize the new churches) and to appoint elders.

4. Sound doctrine.

5. A different doctrine.

6. The sound words of our Lord Jesus Christ .

7. Accords with godliness.

8. The truth.

9. Godliness.

10. His word.

11. The preaching.

12. The command of God.

13. An elder must hold firm to the trustworthy word as taught.

14. This is so the elder can give instruction in sound doctrine and rebuke those who contradict it.

15. Pillar.

16. Buttress.

17. Truth.

18. To the public reading of Scripture, to exhortation, and to teaching.

19. Paul told him to keep a close watch on himself and on his teaching.

20. Declare.

21. Exhort.

22. Rebuke.

23. Authority.

24. Disregard.

25. Works done.

26. Righteousness.

27. Mercy.

28. Grace.

29. Insist.

30. Teach.

31. Sound doctrine.

32. Older men.

33. Older women.

34. Young women.

35. Younger men.

36. Slaves.

37. The rich.

38. Pray.

39. Be submissive.

40. Ungodliness.

41. Worldly passions.

42. Self-controlled.

43. Upright.

44. Godly.

45. Good works.

Paul's Second Epistle to Timothy

2 Timothy

2 Timothy

1. Paul was suffering as a prisoner in chains for having preached the gospel.

2. The word of God was not bound.

3. Paul was not ashamed because he knew whom he had believed (the Lord), and was convinced he was able to keep all that had been entrusted to him.

4. Paul called on Timothy to not be ashamed of the testimony about the Lord; he called on him to share in suffering for the gospel.

5. Paul urged Timothy to follow the pattern of sound words he'd heard from Paul.

6. He called on him to guard the good deposit that had been entrusted to him.

7. All whom Paul had thought would support him had deserted him.

8. Paul found that the Lord stood by him and strengthened him.

9. Paul believed that his imprisonment and trial would end in his execution.

10. Paul asked Timothy to do his best to come to him soon.

11. Paul asked Timothy to bring Mark with him, and his cloak, books, and, "above all," the parchments.

12. Before winter.

13. Paul said all who desire to live a godly life in Christ Jesus will be persecuted.

14. Things Paul said in between two mentions of suffering for Christ: God saved and called him.

    God did this not because of Paul's works but because of God's purpose and grace.

    God planned this salvation before the ages began.

    God accomplished this salvation in Jesus Christ.

    Christ Jesus abolished death and brought life and immortality.

    God had appointed Paul a preacher, apostle, and teacher of the gospel.

15. Paul urged Timothy to be strengthened by the grace of Christ.

16. Timothy was to entrust to faithful men what he had heard from Paul, so those men would also teach it to others.

17. Suffering.

18. A soldier, an athlete, and a farmer.

19. Timothy should remember Christ Jesus, risen from the dead, the offspring of David.

20. Paul urged Timothy to do his best to present himself to God as one approved, a workman that didn't need to be ashamed.

21. The Word of truth (Scripture).

22. Paul told Timothy to continue in what he had learned and had firmly believed.

23. The sacred writings.

24. Make a person wise for salvation.

25. Breathed out.

26. God.

27. Teaching.

28. Reproof.

29. Correction.

30. Training in righteousness.

31. Competent.

32. Every good work.

33. God.

34. Christ Jesus.

35. Preach the Word.

36. In season and out of season.

37. People wouldn't endure sound teaching, but would turn away from listening to the truth.

38. Teachers to suit their own passions.

39. Sober-minded.

40. Enduring.

41. Evangelist.

42. Fulfilling the ministry.

43. Paul said the Lord would rescue him from every evil deed and bring him safely into his heavenly kingdom.

Epistle Review: Part 2

1. 1 Timothy, Titus

2. Galatians

3. Colossians

4. 1–2 Thessalonians

5. Philemon

6. 1–2 Corinthians

7. Ephesians

8. Romans

9. James

10. Philippians

11. 2 Timothy

Test 2
Acts, James, and Paul's Epistles

Matching.

1. Tm

2. J

3. P

4. G

5. Pp

6. J

7. E

8. R

9. Cr

10. T

11. C

12. Th

13. Tm

14. T

15. P

16. Cr

17. G

18. Tm

19. R

Written from prison: Colossians, Ephesians, Philemon, Philippians, 2 Timothy

Short Answer.

20. Jerusalem, all Judea and Samaria, the end of the earth.

21. The Holy Spirit.

22. The rest of the book shows the disciples taking the gospel to all the places Jesus had told them to go.

23. Luke; the Gospel According to Luke.

24. Stephen.

25. Tongues of fire; the sound of a great wind; people speaking in languages they hadn't learned.

26. Peter.

27. Paul.

28. Under house arrest in Rome, still preaching the gospel.

29. Antioch.

30. They left Jerusalem when Stephen was killed and persecution broke out, taking the gospel wherever they went.

31. Jerusalem.

32. Ethiopia.

33. Europe (Macedonia).

34. Hardships faced by Paul: many imprisonments; countless beatings; being often near death; thirty-nine lashes five different times; beatings with rods three times; being stoned; shipwreck three times; being adrift at sea for a day and night; dangers from rivers, from robbers, from the Jews, from Gentiles, from dangers in the city, from dangers in the wilderness, from dangers at sea, and from dangers from false brothers; toil and hardship; many sleepless nights; hunger and thirst; cold and exposure; daily pressure of anxiety for all the churches.

35. Jerusalem

36. Rome

37. Ephesus

38. King Herod

39. Peter

40. James

41. Barnabas

42. Timothy

43. John Mark

The Epistle to the Hebrews

Hebrews 1:1–4:13

1. Many times.
2. Many ways.
3. The prophets.
4. In these last days, God has spoken by his Son.
5. Heir of all things.
6. Created the world.
7. Radiance.
8. Glory.
9. Exact.
10. Nature.
11. Upholds.
12. Word of his power.
13. Purification.
14. At the right hand of God.
15. God's Son.
16. Worship.
17. Ruler.
18. At his right hand.
19. Escape.
20. Neglect.
21. Salvation.
22. Transgression.
23. Disobedience.
24. Jesus partook of flesh and blood.
25. Through death, Jesus destroyed the one who has the power of death, the devil, and delivered those who, through fear of death, were slaves.
26. Propitiation.
27. The sins.
28. Builder.
29. Servant.
30. Son.
31. The writer warned the people not to have an evil, unbelieving heart.
32. Falling away.
33. No one would be hardened by the deceitfulness of sin.
34. Our original confidence.
35. Firm.
36. To the end.

Hebrews 4:14–10:39

1. Like the other priests, Jesus was tempted in every way. Unlike the other priests, he never sinned.
2. The source of eternal salvation.
3. Because they couldn't continue ministering because they died.
4. Forever.
5. Permanently.
6. Jesus is able to save to the uttermost those who draw near to God through him.

7. Daily.

8. Sacrifices for their own sin.

9. Himself once.

10. Promises.

11. Once a year.

12. The blood of bulls and goats.

13. A copy and shadow of the heavenly things.

14. Once.

15. His own blood.

16. Greater.

17. More perfect.

18. Hands.

19. The writer complained that his readers had become dull of hearing.

20. They should be teachers themselves.

21. Basic principles.

22. It would be impossible to restore that person to repentance.

23. Crucify.

24. Contempt.

25. A shadow of the good things to come.

26. Make people perfect.

27. The sacrifices had to be offered continually, every year. If they had made people perfect, they wouldn't need to be offered anymore.

28. They provided a reminder of sins year after year.

29. Take away sins.

30. Offer the same sacrifices.

31. One for all time.

32. Jesus sat down at the right hand of God.

33. By his one offering, Jesus has perfected for all time those being sanctified.

34. Draw near.

35. Hold fast.

36. Wavering.

37. Stir up.

38. Love.

39. Good deeds.

40. Meet together.

41. Encouraging.

42. Go on.

43. Deliberately.

44. Knowledge of the truth.

45. A sacrifice for sins no longer remains for such people.

46. A fearful expectation of judgment and a fury of fire.

47. It is a fearful thing to fall into the hands of the living God.

48. The opposite of shrinking back is having faith.

Hebrews 11–13

Hebrews 11–13

1. Assurance.

2. Hoped for.

3. Conviction.

4. Not seen.

5. By faith.

6. Examples of faith:

Abel	The prophets
Enoch	The Israelites
Noah	Joshua
Abraham	Rahab
Sarah	Gideon
Isaac	Barak
Jacob	Samson
Joseph	Jephthah
Moses' parents	David
Moses	Samuel

7. Wonderful things from the Hebrews 11 list that occurred because of people's faith: kingdoms were conquered, justice was enforced, promises were obtained, lions' mouths were stopped, fire's power was quenched, the sword was escaped, the weak were made strong, people became mighty in war, foreign armies were put to flight, women received back their dead by resurrection.

8. Difficult things from the Hebrews 11 list that people endured by their faith: torture, mocking, flogging, chains, imprisonment, being stoned, being sawn in two, being killed with the sword, going about in animal skins, destitution, affliction, mistreatment, wandering about in deserts and mountains, living in dens and caves.

9. Every weight and sin which clings so closely.

10. With endurance.

11. Jesus.

12. Founder.

13. Perfecter.

14. Jesus endured the cross, despising the shame.

15. Jesus also endured the hostility of sinners against himself.

16. Our good.

17. Share his holiness.

18. The writer warned his readers that they must not fail to obtain the grace of God.

19. Esau.

20. He traded his birthright for a single meal.

21. A changed repentance.

22. An unshakeable kingdom.

23. Reverence and awe.

24. A consuming fire.

25. To let brotherly love continue.

26. Showing hospitality.

27. Those who were in prison (for their faith).

28. Those who were mistreated (for the same reason).

29. In honor.

30. The love of money.

31. The reproach he had endured.

32. A lasting city to come.

33. "I will never leave you nor forsake you."

34. My helper.

35. Fear.

36. Man.

Peter's First Epistle

1. Pontus, Galatia, Cappadocia, Asia, Bithynia.

2. Babylon.

1 Peter 1–5

1 Peter 1–5

1. Born again to a living hope.

2. The grace that was to be given to Christians.

3. Angels.

4. The futile ways inherited from their forefathers.

5. The precious blood of Christ

6. God had called them out of darkness into his marvelous light.

7. Chosen.

8. Priesthood.

9. Holy.

10. Possession.

11. Suffered.

12. Bore our sins.

13. Christ's wounds.

14. The Shepherd and Overseer of their souls.

15. In heaven.

16. Perish.

17. Be defiled.

18. Fade.

19. Guarding them.

20. The genuineness of their faith.

21. Praise.

22. Glory and honor.

23. Surprise.

24. The same kinds of suffering.

25. Cast all their anxieties on God, because he cared for them.

26. Christians' ultimate adversary is the devil; Peter compared him to a roaring lion seeking someone to devour.

27. Christians should resist the devil, firm in their faith.

28. Sufferings.

29. Glory.

30. Christ's sufferings.

31. An example by his suffering.

32. He did not revile in return.

33. He did not threaten.

34. He continued to entrust himself to the One who judges justly.

35. Righteous.

36. Unrighteous.

37. Christ's sufferings.

38. They should rejoice, because they will also share his glory.

39. On the grace they will receive at the revelation (return) of Jesus Christ.

40. Holy, because he who called them is holy.

41. Proclaim his excellencies.

42. Christians must abstain from the passions of the flesh, because they would wage war against their souls.

43. Love each other.

44. Cover a multitude of sins.

45. Use the gifts God has given them to serve each other.

46. Honorable.

47. Glorify God.

48. That the ignorance of foolish people who spoke against them would be silenced.

49. To good and gentle masters.

50. To unjust ones.

51. Respectful.

52. Pure.

53. To make a defense to anyone who asks for a reason for the hope they have. They are to do this with gentleness and respect.

54. Murderer.

55. Thief.

56. Evildoer.

57. Meddler.

58. The name of Christ.

59. Entrust their souls.

60. Faithful Creator.

61. Good.

62. A little while.

63. Restore.

64. Confirm.

65. Strengthen.

66. Establish.

67. Eternal glory.

Peter's Second Epistle

2 Peter 1–3

2 Peter 1–3

1. The Lord Jesus had made clear to Peter that the "putting off of his body"—his death—would be soon.

2. Peter wanted to be sure these Christians would be able to recall these things at any time, after his death.

3. All things that pertain to life and godliness.

4. Believers become partakers of the divine nature through God's great promises.

5. Virtue, knowledge, self-control, steadfastness, godliness, brotherly affection, love.

6. Ineffective or unfruitful if they were increasing in these qualities.

7. He said they would be making their calling and election sure if they practiced these qualities.

8. Christ's majesty.

9. God's voice from heaven calling Jesus his beloved Son.

10. On the holy mountain.

11. The prophetic word.

12. The will of man.

13. God.

14. The Holy Spirit.

15. Five.

16. Adultery.

17. Sin.

18. Greed.

19. They had forsaken the right way, and they had gone astray.

20. Freedom.

21. Slaves of corruption.

22. A dog that returns to its own vomit.

23. A washed sow, returning to the mud.

24. Their own sinful desires.

25. As they were from the beginning of creation.

26. For people to repent and not perish.

27. Like a thief.

28. Lives of holiness and godliness.

29. The error of lawless people.

30. The grace and knowledge of our Lord and Savior Jesus Christ.

The Epistle of Jude

Jude

Jude

1. James.

2. Crept in unnoticed.

3. Pervert.

4. Sensuality.

5. Deny.

6. Your love feasts.

7. Feast with you.

8. Feeding themselves.

9. Contend for the faith.

10. The faith was delivered to the saints once for all.

11. Building themselves up.

12. Praying.

13. Keeping themselves.

14. Waiting.

15. Have mercy on those who doubt.

16. Save those in danger of God's judgment by snatching them out of the fire.

17. Show mercy with fear, hating even the garment stained by the flesh.

18. God is able to keep his people from stumbling and to present them blameless before the presence of his glory with great joy.

The First Epistle of John

1 John 1–5

1 John 1–5

1. Propitiation.

2. Jesus Christ has come in the flesh.

3. The antichrist.

4. God sent Jesus.

5. (His) God's Son.

6. To be the Savior of the world.

7. The person who confesses that Jesus is the Son of God.

8. John said that God is light and there is no darkness in him at all.

9. He lies and doesn't practice the truth.

10. He or she will confess the sin and be forgiven.

11. If they walk in the same way in which he walked.

12. Practices righteousness.

13. If we keep his commandments.

14. A liar.

15. Jesus appeared to take away sins.

16. The person who makes a practice of sinning is of the devil.

17. To destroy the works of the devil.

18. No.

19. Born of God.

20. Cannot.

21. Born of God.

22. The one who does not practice righteousness is not of God, and neither is the one who does not love his brother.

23. He is in the darkness.

24. Because we love the brothers.

25. The one who doesn't love abides in death.

26. The one who hates his brother is a murderer, and no murderer has eternal life abiding in him.

27. You will love the children born of him.

28. He has seen.

29. He has not seen.

30. Love.

31. Loves.

32. By laying down his life for his people.

33. Lay down their lives for each other.

34. If a Christian with this world's goods saw a brother in need, he wouldn't close his heart against him.

35. If anyone loves the world and the things of the world.

36. The one who does the will of God abides forever.

37. Come.

38. Know him.

39. In him.

40. True God.

41. Eternal life.

42. Little children, keep yourselves from idols.

The Second Epistle of John

2 John

1. To the elect lady and her children.

2. Love each other, and keep God's commandments.

3. Watch themselves.

4. Receive false teachers into their homes.

5. Any greeting.

6. Because it would be like taking part in the wicked works of the false teacher.

The Third Epistle of John

3 John

1. The beloved Gaius.

2. These brothers were: strangers to Gaius, on a journey "for the sake of the name" (carrying the gospel to others), accepting nothing from the Gentiles to whom they went.

3. Christians should support such people; that makes us fellow workers for the truth.

4. Demetrius.

5. Diotrephes.

6. Himself.

7. He refused to welcome the brothers.

8. Gaius was not to imitate evil; he was to imitate good.

Test 3

Hebrews, Epistles from Peter, Jude and John

Short answer.

1. The author of Hebrews is unknown.

2. To Jewish Christians.

3. To turn back to the laws, priests, and sacrifices of the old covenant system.

4. Superior to all the old covenant had to offer.

5. Faith

6. Suffering.

7. 2 Peter and Jude are similar because they're about the same false teachers, even using some of the same descriptions.

8. Jude was the brother of James (who wrote the epistle) and half-brother of Jesus.

9. Contend for the faith.

10. True faith that leads to eternal life.

11. Those evidences are: right belief about Jesus Christ, love for God's people, a godly lifestyle, love for God's will above all else.

12. Human.

13. God; man; natures; person.

Short essay.

14. Hebrews taught that . . .

Jesus is superior to angels because . . .

. . . he is a Son.

. . . God commanded the angels to worship the Son.

. . . angels are servants; God made Christ ruler.

. . . angels are spirit only; Christ took on a body as well.

Jesus is superior to Moses because . . .

. . . Moses was part of God's house; Jesus is the builder of the house.

. . . Moses was a faithful servant; Jesus is a faithful Son.

Jesus is superior to old covenant priests because . . .

. . . unlike them, Jesus never sinned.

. . . unlike them, Jesus lives forever.

... Jesus' one sacrifice was enough for all time.

... Jesus mediated a new covenant, with better promises.

... Jesus entered the actual presence of God in heaven with his offering.

Jesus is superior to old covenant sacrifices because ...

... his blood accomplished what those sacrifices only pictured.

... Jesus offered only one sacrifice for all time, not many every day.

Revelation

Revelation 1–5

Revelation 1–5

1. To the seven churches in Asia.

2. John was on the island called Patmos on account of the word of God and the testimony of Jesus.

3. Revelation of Jesus Christ.

4. God.

5. The revelation would show to God's servants the things that must soon take place.

6. Reads aloud the words of this prophecy.

7. Hear it.

8. Keep what is written in it.

9. Alpha.

10. Omega.

11. Is.

12. Was.

13. Is to come.

14. Almighty.

15. Faithful.

16. The dead.

17. Ruler.

18. Like a trumpet.

19. In the midst of seven golden lampstands.

20. The seven churches.

21. Like a son of man.

22. A white robe.

23. With a golden sash.

24. In John's vision, Christ had hair white, like white wool, like snow; eyes like a flame of fire; feet like burnished bronze, and his voice sounded like the roar of many waters.

25. Seven stars.

26. The angels of the seven churches.

27. A sharp two-edged sword.

28. Like the sun shining in all its strength.

29. He fell at his feet like a dead man.

30. The Lord touched him.

31. Fear.

32. Living one.

33. Died.

34. Alive forevermore.

35. Death.

36. Hades.

37. Ephesus.

38. Holds the seven stars and walks among the seven candlesticks.

39. Its work, its toil, its patient endurance, its refusal to bear with those who were evil, the fact that it hadn't grown weary; its hatred of the works of the Nicolaitans (false teachers who lived immorally).

40. Abandoning the love they'd had at first.

41. Grant to eat of the tree of life in the paradise of God.

42. Smyrna.

43. The first and the last, who died and came to life.

44. Being rich (in spite of their poverty), and for enduring through tribulation and persecution.

45. Nothing.

46. Not be hurt by the second death.

47. Pergamum.

48. Has the sharp two-edged sword.

49. Holding fast to his name, even though they dwelt where Satan's throne was and for not denying the faith even when Antipas was killed for it.

50. Some among them held to false teachings that encouraged immorality.

51. Give some of the hidden manna and give a white stone with a new name on it that no one else would know.

52. Thyatira.

53. Has eyes like a flame of fire and feet like burnished bronze.

54. Their works, their love, their faith, their service, their patient endurance, their latter works that exceeded their former works.

55. Tolerating a woman, Jezebel, who was a false teacher and immoral.

56. Give authority over the nations, and give the morning star.

57. Sardis.

58. Has the seven spirits of God and the seven stars.

59. Had not "soiled their garments."

60. They had reputation for being alive when they were dead.

61. Clothe in white; would never blot his name out of the book of life; would confess his name before the Father and the angels.

62. Philadelphia.

63. Is holy and true, who has the key of David, who opens and no one can shut, and who shuts and no one can open.

64. Their works, and for keeping his word and not denying him when it was difficult.

65. Nothing.

66. Make a pillar in the temple of God, write on him the name of God and of the city of God, and write on him Jesus' name.

67. Laodicea.

68. Amen, the faithful and true witness, the beginning of God's creation.

69. Nothing.

70. Being lukewarm, neither hot nor cold; for thinking they had everything when they had nothing; for not being aware of their own spiritual poverty.

71. Grant to sit with him on his throne.

72. John saw a door standing open in heaven.

73. God was seated on a throne.

74. God's holiness.

75. They cast their crowns before God's throne.

76. They say that God is worthy of glory, honor, and power, because all things were created by him, and they all exist by his will.

77. A sealed scroll.

78. It was sealed with seven seals, and no one was worthy to open the scroll or look into it.

79. The Lion of the tribe of Judah could open the scroll because he had conquered.

80. John saw a Lamb, standing as though it had been slain.

81. The four living creatures.

82. The twenty-four elders.

83. Slain.

84. Blood.

85. Ransomed.

86. Tribe.

87. Language.

88. People.

89. Nation

90. A kingdom.

91. Priests.

92. Reign.

93. Angels, myriads of myriads and thousands of thousands of them.

94. Every creature in heaven and on earth and under the earth and in the sea.

Revelation 6–11

Revelation
6–11

1. John saw the Lamb open one of the seals.

2. John saw a rider on a white horse, carrying a bow; he was given a crown, and he came to conquer.

3. A bright red horse.

4. Its rider would take peace away so men would kill each other.

5. A great sword.

6. Black.

7. A pair of scales.

8. It was pale. Its rider's name was Death.

9. Hades followed him.

10. The two were given authority to kill a fourth of mankind; they used sword, famine, pestilence (disease), and wild beasts.

11. With the fifth seal, John saw an altar in heaven; under it were the souls of those who had been slain for the word of God and for the witness they had borne.

12. Sovereign Lord, holy and true.

13. For God to judge and avenge their blood.

14. They were to rest and wait until the number of their brothers would be complete, who would be killed as they had been.

15. Types of people listed in 6:15: kings, great ones, generals, the rich, the powerful, everyone, slave and free.

16. People reacted to God's judgment by trying to hide and by begging rocks and mountains to fall on them.

17. Sealed the servants of God on their foreheads.

18. 144,000.

19. John saw a great multitude.

20. Too great to number.

21. The blood of the Lamb.

22. They were from every nation.

23. These people are before the throne of God, and serve him day and night in his temple.

24. The presence of God.

25. Hunger.

26. Thirst.

27. The sun or scorching heat.

28. Their shepherd.

29. To springs of living water.

30. God will wipe every tear from their eyes.

31. The prayers of the saints were offered to God with the incense.

32. Hail and fire mixed with blood.

33. A burning mountain was thrown into the sea, causing a third of the sea to become blood, killing a third of all sea creatures, and destroying a third of all ships.

34. A great blazing star fell from heaven on rivers and springs. A third of the waters became bitter, causing those who drank them to die.

35. A third of the sun, a third of the moon, and a third of the stars were struck, so that a third of their light was darkened.

36. The shaft of the bottomless pit was opened.

37. Locusts.

38. Crowns.

39. Women's.

40. Human.

41. Lions'.

42. Wings.

43. Scorpions.

44. Only people who did not have the seal of God on their foreheads.

45. Five months.

46. The torment would be so bad that people would long to die without being able to.

47. Twice ten thousand times ten thousand troops (or 200 million).

48. One-third of mankind.

49. The rest of mankind did not repent.

50. God said the nations would trample the holy city for forty-two months.

51. The beast would kill the two witnesses when they had finished their testimony.

52. People came to see their dead bodies lying in the street, refusing to let them be buried and celebrating their deaths.

53. The kingdom of our Lord and of his Christ.

54. He would reign forever and ever.

55. Raged.

56. Wrath.

57. The dead to be judged.

58. Rewarding.

59. Fear.

60. Destroying.

Revelation 12–14

1. A great red dragon stood before the woman, so he could devour her child when it was born.

2. Satan.

3. He was born was a male child who would rule all the nations with a rod of iron.

4. The dragon.

5. The people of God conquer by the blood of the Lamb and by the word of their testimony.

6. Satan had great wrath, because he knew his time was short.

7. The dragon went off to make war on the rest of the woman's offspring.

8. As those who keep the commandment of God and hold to the testimony of Jesus.

9. His power, his throne, and great authority.

10. Exercise authority for forty-two months.

11. Make war on the saints and conquer them.

12. Every tribe and people and language and nation.

13. Those whose names had been written from the foundation of the world in the Lamb's book of life.

14. Like the horns of a lamb.

15. Like a dragon.

16. By the signs (miracles) it's allowed to work.

17. The first beast.

18. Had them slain.

19. People without the mark couldn't buy or sell.

20. Fear.

21. Glory.

22. Worship.

23. Babylon.

24. Fallen.

25. Any who received the mark of the beast or worshiped the beast would drink the full cup of God's wrath and be tormented forever.

Revelation 15–18

Revelation 15–18

1. John said these would be the last, because in them the wrath of God would be finished.

2. Those who had conquered the beast.

3. Almighty.

4. King.

5. Nations.

6. Great.

7. Amazing.

8. Just.

9. True.

10. Fear.

11. Glorify.

12. Holy.

13. Come.

14. Worship.

15. They developed harmful, painful sores.

16. The sea became like the blood of a corpse and every living thing in the sea died.

17. They became blood.

18. The fourth angel poured out his bowl on the sun, and it scorched people with fire.

19. People responded by cursing God; they did not repent and give him glory.

20. On the throne of the beast, and his kingdom was plunged into darkness.

21. People cursed the God of heaven for their pain and sores and didn't repent of their deeds.

22. The way for kings to come.

23. For battle against God.

24. The great city split into three parts.

25. The cities of other nations fell.

26. 100 pounds.

27. The people cursed God for the plague of the hail.

28. The woman was dressed in purple and scarlet, adorned with gold, jewels, and pearls.

29. Abominations and the impurities of her sexual immorality.

30. Become drunk.

31. Her name was "Babylon the great, mother of prostitutes and of earth's abominations."

32. The blood of the saints, the martyrs of Jesus.

33. Because God had put it into their hearts to carry out his purpose.

34. In a single day.

35. Mighty.

36. In a single hour.

Revelation 19–22

1. Judged.

2. The marriage of the Lamb.

3. His Bride.

4. Faithful and True.

5. He would judge and make war in righteousness.

6. Many crowns.

7. His robe was dipped in blood.

8. The Word of God.

9. The armies of heaven followed the rider on the white horse.

10. He would strike down the nations.

11. On his robe and thigh was written the name King of kings and Lord of lords.

12. The beast and the kings of the earth with their armies.

13. The beast and the false prophet were captured and thrown alive into the lake of fire.

14. They were slain by the sword that came from the rider's mouth.

15. An angel bound the dragon with a great chain, threw him into the pit, and sealed it. The dragon is also called "that ancient serpent, the devil, and Satan."

16. The dragon would be left there 1000 years, and the result would be that he couldn't deceive the nations.

17. Deceived.

18. Gathered.

19. Battle.

20. Their number was as the sand of the sea.

21. Fire came down from heaven and consumed them.

22. The devil was thrown into the lake of fire, where the beast and the false prophet were.

23. Forever.

24. People were judged according to what they had done.

25. Book of life.

26. As a bride adorned for her husband.

27. God.

28. Man.

29. Dwell.

30. Their God.

31. His people.

32. The holy city Jerusalem.

33. The glory of God.

34. A most rare jewel.

35. Tears.

36. Death.

37. Mourning.

38. Crying.

39. Pain.

40. Temple.

41. Temple.

42. Sun.

43. Moon.

44. Light.

45. Lamp.

46. Night.

47. Unclean.

48. Detestable.

49. False.

50. Accursed.

51. The glory and the honor of the nations.

52. The river of the water of life.

53. The throne of God.

54. The tree of life.

55. The healing of the nations.

56. The throne of God and of the Lamb.

57. See.

58. Face.

59. Coming soon.

60. Kept the prophecy of the book.

61. Blessed.

62. His recompense.

63. Repay.

64. On those who wash their robes.

65. The right to eat from the tree of life, and may enter the city.

66. John warned against adding to or taking away from what was in this prophecy.

67. Amen. Come, Lord Jesus!

Test 4
Revelation

Short answer.

1. Revelation was addressed to seven churches in Asia: churches in Ephesus, Smyrna, Perga-mum, Thyatira, Sardis, Philadelphia, and Laodicea.

2. The people who received Revelation faced persecution, false teaching, and temptation.

3. "Apocalypse" means "unveiling."

4. This word is an accurate description of Revelation, because the book pulls back the curtain to show what is going on behind the scenes that causes events in our world, and because it pulls back the veil to show what will happen in the future.

5. The apostle John wrote Revelation. He was on the island of Patmos. He'd been exiled for preaching the gospel.

6. John's main intention in writing Revelation was to encourage the churches to stand firm and resist the persecution, false teaching, and temptation they faced.

7. We can be sure the main purpose of Revelation was not to give exact details about what would happen at the end of time because that would not have been at all helpful to the persecuted, struggling Christians of the first century.

8. Revelation's idea of only two kinds of people, God's people and God's enemies, fulfilled what God said in the garden of Eden: there would be enmity between the offspring of the woman and the offspring of the Serpent.

9. Revelation shows us that behind the persecution of God's people by their enemies is Satan's hatred for God.